Asia Bibi is currently in prison in Pakistan awaiting the result of her appeal against the death sentence she was given in 2009. Her family have had to go into hiding.

D0544226

BLASPHEMY

The True, Heartbreaking Story of a Woman Sentenced to Death over a Cup of Water

Asia Bibi

With Anne-Isabelle Tollet

virago

VIRAGO

First published in Great Britain in 2012 by Virago Press

Copyright © Oh! Editions, 2011. All rights reserved.

The moral right of the author has been asserted.

Some names within the text have been changed.

A CIP catalogue record for this book
is available from the British Library.

ISBN 978-1-84408-888-1

Typeset in Bembo by M Rules
Printed and bound in Great Britain by
Clays Ltd, St Ives plc

Papers used by Virago are from well-managed forests
and other responsible sources.

MIX
Paper from
responsible sources
FSC® C104740

Virago Press
An imprint of
Little, Brown Book Group
100 Victoria Embankment
London EC4Y 0DY

An Hachette UK Company
www.hachette.co.uk

www.virago.co.uk

Contents

	Preface	vii
	Foreword	xx
1	A Black Hole	1
2	Blasphemy	11
3	I Can No Longer See the Stars	25
4	Death by Hanging	41
5	The Christian Minister	55
6	Happy Christmas	67
7	The Pope's Message	81
8	They Kill the Governor	93
9	They Kill the Minister	105
	Afterword	135

Preface

This is the true story of an extraordinary friendship between two very different women, brought together as a result of human cruelty.

I am a French journalist for an international news channel and spent three years, 2008–2011, living in Pakistan. Asia Bibi is a Pakistani wife and mother living under sentence of death. Since 2009 she has been in prison in Sheikhupura, in the province of Punjab, where she is held in appalling conditions unworthy of a democracy. Her crime? She's a Christian who drank a cup of water from a well used by her Muslim friends. This story sounds unlikely, but it really is true. Asia was arrested, tried and sentenced to hang for the crime of blasphemy. Since then, she has never stopped proclaiming her innocence from the depths of her windowless prison cell.

I was never allowed to visit Asia in prison, but despite this we got to know each other very well. Without ever meeting, or talking directly, we were able to form an unbreakable friendship.

I first came across Asia Bibi's name in the local Pakistani press, the day after she was sentenced to death in November 2010. With the support of my friend Shahbaz Bhatti, then Pakistani Minister for Minorities, I did a number of reports on her case for various television news programmes. At that time Asia's family were living under Bhatti's protection, and he enabled me to meet them. For a few days Asia's case shocked the world – and then it was forgotten. It was at this point that I realised that the only way to help her was to write a book.

Before starting, I talked the whole thing over at great length with Asia's family, her lawyer and Shahbaz Bhatti, who, as well as being Minister for Minorities, was also a Christian, later murdered by the Taliban, on 2 March 2011, for his public support for Asia. We all came to the same conclusion: Asia was in an impossible situation, she had been sentenced to death by her own country, there was a price on her head and her family were in hiding, also threatened with death by religious fanatics. This book could save her.

But for Asia's version of events to be heard beyond the

walls of her cell, we had to take on the Pakistani authorities, who didn't want her story to be known outside Pakistan and were fiercely opposed to the idea that I should meet her. They were horrified by the prospect of a French woman taking an interest in this wife and mother walled up alive in a filthy cell in the Punjab. No, no one must hear Asia Bibi proclaim her innocence as she waited in appalling conditions for her own execution.

Though we were not allowed to meet, I was not prepared to give up the idea of writing this book. So I managed to talk to Asia through her husband Ashiq, who is the only person apart from her lawyer allowed to visit her in prison, once a week. For two months I would wait for Ashiq at the prison gate and there, with the help of an Urdu–English interpreter, he would tell me Asia's answers to my questions.

In this roundabout way Asia and I developed a special understanding that goes far beyond ordinary friendship.

She was the voice, I was the pen.

My manuscript was read to Asia in prison by her lawyer in a series of visits. This had to be done in total secret, as even the idea of this book was dangerous in Pakistan. Hearing her story read out made Asia very happy. To show her enthusiasm she asked her lawyer to sign every page of the book, as a mark of her total approval. Her dark, filthy cell was lit by a glimmer of hope.

Asia Bibi is the only woman this century to have been condemned to death for blasphemy. Her lawyer appealed against the decision, but until the date for the hearing is set by the High Court in Lahore, Asia risks being murdered at any time, or simply dying of exhaustion. A mullah in Peshawar has offered a reward of 5,000 euros to anyone who kills Asia. This sum is a fortune in Pakistan.

Asia's case has shed light on Pakistan's blasphemy law, which has seen thousands of innocent people sentenced to prison for reasons that have nothing to do with religious discrimination. It is vital to stress that most victims of this law are Muslims.

The law against blasphemy is unjust. It is used to settle disputes between neighbours or to get rid of a rival simply by making an oral accusation against them.

Through no fault of her own, Asia Bibi has become a symbol of this law. The fanatics are doing all they can to keep the law in place and have turned the case of this powerless young woman into a challenge to the government.

Yet we all know that the Islam advocated by the fundamentalists bears little resemblance to the great religion upheld by Muslims for centuries. In surat 5 of verse 32, the Koran teaches that anyone who kills an innocent person kills all humankind, and anyone who saves a life saves all humankind.

Asia Bibi is innocent. The Pakistani government knows this, but does nothing for fear of reprisals. In 2010 Pakistan ratified the International Covenant on Civil and Political Rights. Yet in refusing to act and to pass the necessary reforms, the state has become an accomplice of the fundamentalists. The country's international undertakings are not compatible with keeping the crime of blasphemy on its statute books.

Pakistan is a great nation and Pakistanis are great people. They are friendly and hospitable and the Islam they follow is a religion that welcomes others, as I know from my own experience. In a population of 180 million, there is only a handful of extremists. But, by instilling terror, those few extremists are holding back the development of the entire country. I am glad that, by giving lectures throughout the world, I am able to give a voice to civil society in Pakistan, to the many people and groups who are currently unable to speak freely without fear of attack. If we manage to free Asia, we will be helping others unjustly imprisoned by this law.

Today Asia Bibi no longer has a lawyer; no one dares represent her for fear of being killed.

This book is now her only hope of survival. But time is

passing, her health is deteriorating, her husband risks being killed every time he visits her and her children cannot see their mother for their own safety. So her husband and five children are also suffering from the accusation of blasphemy. They are all living with the threat of death and have gone into hiding, frequently moving house and unable to go outside or to work. The children miss their mother badly and have stopped going to school for their own safety. The youngest is only ten years old.

Through this book, which provides them with royalties, Asia now has enough to eat and her disabled daughter is able to receive costly medical treatment.

When you read this book you will understand that Asia Bibi is not just a symbol, but a real, generous woman, forty-two years old and the mother of five children. Her sixteen-year-old daughter Sidra says, 'Our life stopped when Mum went away. My sisters and I cry every day because we miss her so much. We don't know if she will ever come back; we're very afraid of what might happen.' Sidra's face is worn by anxiety. She can't understand why her family has become the target of so much hate. 'We've always had Muslim friends; being Christians was never a problem for us and we've always respected Islam. I want to be a doctor but since Mum's been in prison we've had death threats too and I can't go to school.'

The publication of this book represents a first victory,

but the fight is only just beginning. In the name of religious freedom we must ensure that Asia is released and can at last return to her family. If we can raise her case with the politicians in our own countries and join together in an international chain of solidarity, we will be able to save Asia Bibi.

Personally, I'm looking forward to the day when I can give my friend Asia a big hug to celebrate her return to freedom.

Foreword

I'm writing to you from my prison cell in Sheikhupura, Pakistan. These are the last days of my life – maybe even the last hours. That's what I was told by the court that sentenced me to death.

I'm afraid.

Afraid for my own life and for the lives of my children and my husband. They're suffering too. Through me, my whole family has been sentenced. My faith is strong and I pray to my merciful God to protect us. I long to see their smiling eyes again. But I don't think I'll live long enough to see that day.

The extremists will never leave us alone.

I haven't killed or robbed anyone, but in the eyes of my country's justice system I've done something much worse: I have blasphemed. It's the crime of crimes, the supreme insult.

I'm accused of having spoken ill of the Prophet. It's an accusation that can be used against anyone, whatever their religion or opinions.

My name is Aasiya Noreen Bibi. I'm a 'nobody', as they say around here – a simple country woman from Ittan Wali, a tiny village in Punjab province, in central Pakistan. But today my name is known around the world.

Everyone's heard of 'Asia' Bibi.

I've never blasphemed. I'm innocent. I've never committed a crime in my whole life.

I want to tell the whole world that I respect the Prophet. I'm a Christian and I believe in my God, but everyone should be free to choose what they believe in.

For the last three years I've been locked up, unable to speak out. Now I want to have my say. I want the truth to be heard.

Salman Taseer, Governor of Punjab, and Shahbaz Bhatti, the Minister for Minorities, both died because they supported me. They were killed by fundamentalists. It was terrible – they were slaughtered more cruelly than if they were animals. When I think of their families it makes me cry.

As Salman Taseer said, 'In the Pakistan of our founding fathers, this blasphemy law did not exist.'

Thanks to my beloved husband Ashiq and other people

I can't name for their own safety, I can write to you today, from this cell where I'm buried alive.

I'm asking you for help. Please don't forget about me.

I need you.

1

A Black Hole

In prison the nights and days are all the same.

From time to time I doze, without ever really feeling like I've been asleep. As I drift off the sounds of the prison pull me back. A door bangs: the warders are changing shift. Clinking keys, footsteps and the squeak of the soup-trolley wheels mean it's meal-time. A metal bucket clangs on the tiles in the corridor, so it's time for the evening chores – or maybe it's the morning chores. Mine is a slow death, painless so far, but so slow …

I can't really say what I feel. Fear, definitely. The fear is always there, but it doesn't shake me up the way it did at first.

Back then it used to set my heart thumping in my chest. Now I'm calmer; I've stopped being so jumpy all the time. I still have my tears: they flow often enough, but I'm done with sobbing. My tears are my cellmates. They remind me that I haven't completely given up, that I'm a victim of injustice. They remind me that I'm innocent.

The court in Nankana didn't just throw me in here, into this cold, damp cell, so small I can reach out and touch the walls on both sides; it also took away my right to see my five children. Never again will I hold them close and tell them the tales of ogres and Punjabi princes that my mother told me when I was their age.

This evening, and every evening, their absence is far more cruel to me than prison. Not being able to touch them, to smell them. I'd give everything I have for a moment with them, at home, all six of us in the family bed. I laugh when I think of our endless delousing sessions last winter, when Isham, my youngest daughter, used to hide in the laundry basket trying to get away from the nit comb.

Ashiq, my husband, solemnly told the children that we had to be careful because a louse that was fed on little girl's skin might one day grow as big as a rat.

Isham screamed. 'A rat? In my hair?' And she ran to hide under my tunic.

My God, how I loved moments like that.

And talking of my God, by whose will I'm in this prison now, how long will He make me suffer? I was a good Christian before all this, and the fact that my children miss me so much means I must have been a good mother.

So why am I being punished? My husband found me as pure as the Virgin Mary on our wedding night. And every Christmas after that his mother used to congratulate him for marrying me. I was a good wife, a good mother and a good Christian, but now it seems I'm good only to hang.

I don't know much about the world outside my village – I've had no education – but I do know the difference between right and wrong. I'm not a Muslim, but I am a good Pakistani, a Catholic and a patriot. I love my country as I love my God. We have plenty of Muslim friends who have never treated us as different. And even though life hasn't always been easy for us, we had our place and we were happy to keep to it. Of course, when you're a Christian in Pakistan, you have to keep your head down. Some people see us as second-class citizens. We get the jobs no one else wants, the lowly jobs. But I was happy with my lot. Before all this business began I was happy with my family, back home in Ittan Wali.

Now it's been decided I'm to be hanged, lots of people have come to see me – important people, and foreigners too. At least they did at first, but now I've been put in solitary confinement. Now I can't see anyone but my husband and my lawyer.

I still don't really understand who all those visitors were, but they helped me just the same. Apparently people in other countries find it hard to believe that here in Pakistan thugs, murderers and rapists get better treatment than those accused of insulting the Koran or the Prophet Muhammad. But I've always known this. For a Christian to express the slightest doubt about Islam means dying on the scaffold – but only after a long stay in prison.

These days I see nothing but bars, wet ground and walls black with filth. Everything smells of grease, sweat and urine – it's a disgusting mix, even for a farmer's daughter. I thought I'd get used to it, but no. It's the smell of death mixed with despair.

I'm a country girl, raised among the sugar-cane fields. The first time my husband touched me, he told me my skin tasted like sugar cane. I burst out laughing. My mother had told me that's what all the village boys say the first time, and no one knows where they get such a weird idea. All the girls used to laugh about it. We used to imagine the boys sitting in a classroom, in front of a blackboard, being shown how girls are made. One of us would pretend to be the teacher:

'But make sure you remember to tell them their skin tastes like sugar cane ...'

We were fifteen years old at most, but already everyone knew I was different. There were a lot of times when I'd be left out of whatever my Muslim friends were doing. During Ramadan, for example, I used to drink in secret during the days when they weren't allowed to eat or drink anything at all between sunrise and sunset.

Those days didn't seem so far away until I was put in prison. I was still one of them back then – different, but still part of their group.

Now I'm like all the other blasphemers in Pakistan. Guilty or not, their world has been turned upside-down. The lucky ones have their lives destroyed by years of prison. But more often those who have committed the supreme offence – Christians, Hindus and Muslims alike – are killed in their cells by a fellow prisoner, or even by a warder. And even if they're eventually acquitted, which very rarely happens, they are always killed when they're released from jail.

In my country the mark of blasphemy can never be wiped clean. To be suspected is a crime in itself in the eyes of the religious fanatics who judge, pass sentence and kill in the name of God. Yet Allah is nothing but love. I really don't understand why people use religion to do evil. I believe we are simply men and women first, and followers of a religion second.

It's become a real problem for me that I don't know how to read and write. It's only now that I realise what an obstacle it is. If I knew how to read, maybe I wouldn't even be locked up in here. I would almost certainly have had more control over things. But instead I've always been on the receiving end, and still am. According to the journalists, ten million Pakistanis would be willing to kill me with their own hands. A mullah in Peshawar has even promised a fortune – 500,000 rupees – to anyone who takes my life. That's enough to buy a big house here, with at least three rooms and every modern convenience. I don't understand why they hate me so much. I've always respected Islam, as my parents and grandparents taught me. In fact, I was happy for my children to learn to read the Muslim holy book in our little village primary school.

I'm the victim of a cruel, collective injustice.

I've been locked up, handcuffed and chained for two years, banished from the world and waiting to die. I don't know how long I've got left to live. Every time my cell door opens my heart beats faster. My life is in God's hands and I don't know what's going to happen to me. It's a brutal, cruel existence. But I am innocent. Asia Bibi is innocent; I'm guilty only of being presumed guilty. I'm starting to wonder whether being a Christian in Pakistan today is not just a failing, or a mark against you, but actually a crime.

But though I'm kept in a tiny, windowless cell, I want my voice and my anger to be heard. I want the whole world to know that I'm going to be hanged for helping my neighbour. I'm guilty of having shown someone sympathy. What did I do wrong? I drank water from a well belonging to Muslim women, using 'their' cup, in the burning heat of the midday sun.

I, Asia Bibi, have been sentenced to death because I was thirsty. I'm a prisoner because I used the same cup as those Muslim women, because water served by a Christian woman was regarded as unclean by my stupid fellow fruit-pickers.

Dear God, I don't understand! Why are You putting me through all this?

Here in my grim prison, I want people to hear my small voice denouncing this injustice and barbarity. I want all those who'd like to see me dead to know that for years I worked for a couple of rich Muslim officials. I want to tell those who condemn me that the members of that family, who are good Muslims, didn't have a problem with the fact that a Christian woman was preparing their meals and doing their dishes. I spent six years of my life with them; they are a second family to me, and they love me like a daughter!

I'm full of anger against the blasphemy law that has caused the death of too many Ahmadis, Christians, Hindus and even Muslims.

For too long this law has thrown innocents like me into prison.

Why do the politicians let it happen? Only Governor Salman Taseer and the Minister for Minorities Shahbaz Bhatti have had the courage to support me in public and to oppose this law from a bygone age. A law that is in itself blasphemous, since it causes oppression and death in the name of God.

Those two brave men were gunned down in the street for condemning this injustice. One was a Muslim, the other a Christian. They both knew their lives were at risk, because they had received death threats from the religious fanatics. Nevertheless, those humane, courageous men kept up their fight for religious freedom so that Christians, Muslims and Hindus could live happily together, side by side, in the land of Islam. Those two men paid the supreme price. Perhaps the fact that a Muslim and a Christian spilled their own blood in the same cause is also a message of hope.

But the government is terrified and does whatever the

fundamentalists tell it. According to Ashiq, this accursed law against blasphemy will never be changed. So it will go on taking the lives of many innocent people.

I have to go back to court, to appeal against my death sentence. But I have no confidence in this justice system that lashes out against poor people like me who have nothing. If, by some miracle, I'm not killed in my cell before my appeal is heard, I'll end up murdered anyway.

Without wanting to, I, a poor farmer's daughter, have become an affair of state.

Through no fault of my own, I, Asia Bibi, am now the symbol of the law against blasphemy.

I feel as though I've fallen into a deep black hole with no possible way out. So I wait fearfully for my time to come. If I'm acquitted, my life won't be worth much in Pakistan. I'll have to be adopted by some other country, since my own no longer wants me. I'm condemned to flee my beloved native land, but the fury I've built up in prison over the last two years has given me the strength to want to go on living, abroad, with my family, who are also threatened with death.

No one here is listening to me, so I hope with all my heart that my small voice will be heard outside of Pakistan. My life is not worth much and the religious fundamentalists won't be satisfied until they have exacted their cruel punishment. But I also want my story to be useful to others like me, who are unjustly condemned in the name of this law.

I beg the Virgin Mary to help me bear another minute without my children, who are wondering why their mum has suddenly left home.

Each day God gives me the strength to bear this horrible injustice, but how much longer can I go on? Months? Years – always assuming I'm given that much time to live? I pray to the Lord every day to help me survive long enough to see the end of this miserable existence, but I can feel myself getting weaker. I haven't got the strength I had before and I don't know how much longer I can stand up to all the bullying I suffer and the appalling conditions I'm living in.

2

Blasphemy

My life fell apart one Sunday in June.

It should have been just another day like all the rest. When I woke up that morning, I could never have imagined it was a day that would change my life for ever. That day, 14 June 2009, is imprinted on my memory. I can still see every detail.

That morning I got up earlier than usual, to take part in the big falsa-berry harvest. I'd been told about it by Farah, our lovely local shopkeeper:

'Why don't you go falsa-picking tomorrow in that field

just outside the village? You know the one: it belongs to the Nadeems, the rich family who live in Lahore. The pay is two hundred and fifty rupees.'

'Thanks very much, Farah, I'll do that,' I said, going off with my bag of spices.

Because it was Sunday, Ashiq wasn't working in the brickworks. It was his well-deserved day off. While I was getting ready to go to work he was still fast asleep in the big family bed with two of our daughters, who were also worn out after a long week at school. I looked at them all with love before I left the room, and thanked God for giving me such a wonderful family.

I tried to open the door very carefully, so as not to make too much noise, because for a few days the lock had been sticking. I'd asked Ashiq to oil it, but he always forgot to do the things I asked unless I said them several times. There was a scraping noise as I tried to undo the lock. Then, *bang!*, the door opened, but no one woke up, despite the noise. A good thing too. Ashiq worked all week at the brickworks from sunrise to sunset. It was very hard, particularly in the stifling June heat.

He seemed a bit tired just then; I hoped he would get some of his strength back before starting work again the next day. I was very proud that Ashiq made bricks. His boss often used to say to his dozen workers:

'You are the pillars of the construction industry. By

making bricks all day you're helping to build buildings and make Pakistan great!'

So Ashiq was doing work that was important for our country. When he started the job, I could never understand why he always came home in the evening with his feet more dirty than his hands.

'Why are your feet always all black, Ashiq? If you're working as a mason it should be your hands that get dirty.'

Ashiq laughed and laughed. He teased me because I didn't know how to make bricks.

I was annoyed. I said, 'Of course I don't, why would I? It's not women's work and my father was a farmer and so were my uncles. They spent all day in the fields. So how do you expect me to know how to make bricks?'

Ashiq was touched by my confession of ignorance. He held my hand and explained:

'When I get to the brickworks, I start by collecting earth in a big wheelbarrow. You can see there's always a huge pile of earth next to where we make the bricks. Then we mix the earth with sand in a huge vat. You have to be really careful to make sure there's the same amount of sand and earth. Now I'll tell you why I always come home with black feet. To make sure the earth and sand are really well mixed, I climb into the vat and mix it all up with my feet. I squash it and squeeze it till it's like a kind of paste. The mixture has to be soft, so we have to tread it for a really long time.'

I was amazed by what Ashiq was telling me.

'So that's why your feet are all black … Go on, go on!' I said, like a child listening to a story.

'Then I put the paste into a mould and leave it to dry in the sun for a few hours. When it's dry I put the mould in an underground kiln and it gets fired overnight. The next day, when I get it out of the kiln, I've got a brick!'

I like it when people take the trouble to explain something to me, and Ashiq described all the details so well. I'd never have thought brick-making would be so interesting.

'How do you dry the moulds when it's raining?'

'We try to dry them under a shelter when it rains. But it takes much, much longer and sometimes the water gets into the bricks before they dry. If that happens we have to start all over again.'

I was impressed by the skill he needed to do his work. All I know how to do is pick fruit. I'd never be able to make bricks, no matter how much Ashiq explained.

When I left the house it was still early, but already it was very hot. I would rather have stayed at home to spend some time with Ashiq and the children. To cheer myself up, I thought about the 250 rupees I'd get at the end of the day. For people like us, who aren't rich, 250 rupees is a lot.

With that much money I'd be able to buy two kilos of flour, enough to make chapatis for the whole family for a week.

The village was almost deserted, apart from some little children sitting on a brick wall, enthusiastically repeating verses from the Koran that they'd learned the day before in their little madrasah. I smiled at them and went on my way through the silent streets.

Ittan Wali is very run-down. The rough streets are full of holes. The stream that runs through our village could be lovely if it wasn't actually an open sewer. Often the smell that comes off it is not very nice, particularly in the hot season, but I was used to it. It was the smell of my home. Our village is very poor, but the madrasah had recently been renovated. Farah the shopkeeper, who took her son Zoeb there every week after Friday prayers, told me it looked like new.

'Shame you can't go, Asia, you should see it! It's all painted white with lots of little blue tiles. It's really beautiful.'

I thought to myself that it would be good if the next time something got renovated in our village it was the sewers.

That day the road leading to the fruit-picking seemed to go on for ever. Around me the land stretched away all flat and monotonous to the horizon and the ground was cracked by drought. When I looked up I almost bumped into a woman whose face was covered by a worn veil. She stretched out her hand. She was carrying a bowl and a filthy child and she really did look very poor. Without speaking she waved her hand in front of my face, then a little shamefully pulled back her veil. What I saw really shocked me: her features had literally melted. Her skin had been burned and eaten away. She seemed to be almost blind. I understood. More than half her face had been destroyed by acid.

'Who did that to you?'

'My husband. He threw acid over me while I was asleep, just like that, for no reason. It was a long time ago now.'

I felt really sorry and sad for her, but I had nothing to give her, not even an orange. I looked round and pointed towards the village a few hundred metres behind.

'Come and see me tomorrow. I'll be able to give you something then. My house is on the corner with a blue iron gate. Ask for Asia's house.'

She tapped her head lightly to say thank you, then set off again in the opposite direction from me.

Then at last I saw the field that was to be harvested. Around fifteen women were already at work, picking away, bent double, their backs half hidden by the tall bushes. It was going to be a physically exhausting day in such heat, but I needed those 250 rupees. Some of the women greeted me with a smile. I recognized my neighbour, Musarat, who was the seamstress in my village. I gave her a little wave, but she turned back to the bushes again at once. Musarat wasn't really an agricultural worker and I didn't often see her in the fields, so I realized times must be hard for her family. In the end it was just our lot to be poor, all of us. Whenever I went out of my house and walked past hers, her green gate was always a little open. I used to see her sitting there sewing all day in her yard, with her old sewing machine, surrounded by chickens. I didn't think Musarat was a bad person, but she was known for being an old gossip who always wanted to know what was going on outside.

A hard-faced woman dressed in clothes that had been mended many times came over to me with an old yellow bowl.

'If you fill the bowl you get two hundred and fifty rupees,' she said without really looking at me.

I looked at the huge bowl and thought I would never finish before sunset. Looking at the other women's bowls, I also realized mine was much bigger. They were reminding me that I'm a Christian. That kind of thing happens all the time. Christians often get paid less than Muslims for the same work. Luckily Ashiq didn't suffer that kind of injustice. He used to get his 6,000 rupees at the brick-works, the same as the Muslims. His boss treated everyone the same.

It takes a lot of care and attention to pick falsa. To do it properly you have to make sure you pick the tiny dark red berries cleanly, without bruising them. It's very hard work. You have to push your way through the thorny bushes to pick the fruit off the tips of the twigs. I pulled on the branches, getting scratched pretty much every time, and very, very carefully I picked the little berries one by one, trying not to get caught on the thorns. I went on and on, making the same movements over and over for what seemed like for ever, but when I looked down at my bowl I realized it was only half full. Despite the care I'd taken, my hands were scratched raw and my fingertips were wet and red – they looked as though I'd dipped them in a paint pot. The sun was beating down, and by midday it was like working in an oven. I was dripping with sweat and I could hardly think or move for the suffocating heat. In my mind I could see the river beside my village. If only I could have jumped into that cool water!

But since the river was nowhere near I freed myself from my bushes and walked over to the nearby well. Already I could sense the coolness rising up from its old stone depths, and leaned over the edge to see if there was any water down there.

Every time I used to lean over a well I'd be reminded of a terrible tragedy that happened when I was a little girl. I was nine years old when my Aunt Noor came rushing into my parents' house in a terrible state:

'Have you seen Shan?' she asked my mum in a panicky voice.

'No. Have you seen him, Asia?'

Shan was my little cousin. He was three years old.

'No, what's happened?'

My aunt was in floods of tears.

'He's been missing for over an hour now, and no one knows where he is. No one has seen him.'

The men and women of the village looked for him all night, but they couldn't find him. The next morning one of the women went to the well and saw Shan's little body floating deep down in the darkness. No one had thought to look there. I used to think of that tragedy every time I filled a bucket with water. It left its mark on me and I wouldn't let my children go near the well in our village, even my big girl of thirteen.

I look at my fellow pickers, heads and hands buried in the bushes or in their bowls. They look so busy with their work. Despite the heat they're still going at it with the same energy they had at the start.

I pull up a bucketful of water and dip in the old metal

cup resting on the side of the well. The cool water is all I can think of. I gulp it down and I feel better; I pull myself together.

Then I start to hear muttering. I pay no attention and fill the cup again, this time holding it out to a woman next to me who looks like she's in pain. She smiles and reaches out … At exactly that moment Musarat pokes her ferrety nose out from the bush, her eyes full of hate:

'Don't drink that water, it's *haram*!'

I jump out of my skin and tip the water out before the woman has had time to take it. Musarat addresses all the pickers, who have suddenly stopped work at the sound of the word '*haram*'.

'Listen, all of you, this Christian has dirtied the water in the well by drinking from our cup and dipping it back in several times. Now the water is unclean and we can't drink it! Because of her!'

It's so unfair that for once I decide to defend myself and stand up to the old witch.

'I think Jesus would see it differently from Muhammad.'

Musarat is furious. 'How dare you think for the Prophet, you filthy animal!'

Three other women start shouting even louder.

'That's right, you're just a filthy Christian! You've contaminated our water and now you dare to speak for our

Prophet! Stupid bitch, your Jesus didn't even have a proper father, he was a bastard, don't you know that? Muhammad had a proper father who acknowledged him, his name was Abdullah. Ever heard of Abdullah? Jesus was unclean, just like you.'

I stand my ground.

'That's not true. Go and ask the village mullah.'

Musarat comes over as though she's going to hit me and yells:

'You should convert to Islam to redeem yourself for your filthy religion.'

I feel a pain deep inside. We Christians have always stayed silent: we've been taught since we were babies never to say anything, to keep quiet because we're a minority. But I'm stubborn too and now I want to react, I want to defend my faith. I don't want to let these women attack my religion in such an insulting way.

I take a deep breath to fill my lungs with courage.

'I'm not going to convert. I believe in my religion and in Jesus Christ, who died on the cross for the sins of mankind. What did your Prophet Muhammad ever do to save mankind? And why should it be me that converts instead of you?'

That's when the hatred bursts out from all sides. All around me the women start screaming.

'How dare you say such a thing about our Prophet!

You're nothing! You're just a piece of filth, you don't deserve to live! You're nothing and your children are the same! You'll pay dearly for what you've just said about our holy Prophet!'

All this spite and loathing upsets me, but I come back at them.

'I didn't say anything bad, I just asked you a question.'

One of them grabs my bowl and tips the berries into her own. Another one shoves me and Musarat spits in my face with all the scorn she can manage. A foot lashes out and they push me. I fall down. They laugh.

'Bitch! Filthy whore! You've had it now!'

I look at their burning, hate-filled eyes and suddenly I find the strength to jump up. I run home as fast as my legs will carry me. Even when I'm a long way away from them, I can still hear them complaining about me.

As I come in through the blue gate I see Ashiq oiling the lock on the bedroom door. I'm crying so hard I can hardly breathe. Ashiq puts down his bottle of oil and comes over.

'Whatever's the matter, Asia?'

Between sobs I tried to get my breath back and I tell him the whole story: the well, the women, the water that was unclean because I drank from the cup, the outpourings of hate, the insults and blows. I am sobbing really hard and Ashiq tells me to go inside and lie down. He sits beside me and strokes my hair to calm me down.

'Don't worry, it's all over now. Don't think about it any more. I'm sure they've already forgotten all about it.'

Despite Ashiq's comforting words, the torrent of abuse they threw at me keeps going through my head and I can't shake it off. I just keep on sobbing.

Eventually I fall asleep with my husband's hand on my face.

3

I Can No Longer See the Stars

I woke up covered in sweat.

I was cold and I didn't feel good. It was still dark, but I couldn't get back to sleep. Ashiq and the children were fast asleep. I sat up in our family bed, my head filled with images of the fruit harvest: Musarat with her heart full of hate, the fury of the other women, their terrible insults as they spat at me and hit me.

The call of the muezzin rang out, so it was half past five. I used to like hearing the call to prayer five times a day. Even though I didn't go to the mosque, it told me where I was in my day. I knew when it was time to go home to prepare a meal, or when it was time to pick up the children from school. That morning the mullah seemed to be on form. He was singing in tune; it sounded nice. Although I'm Catholic, I liked to be soothed by the verses from the Koran. Ashiq and I would sometimes catch ourselves laughing when the mullah sang the wrong notes or when, at midday on Friday when the most important prayers are said, he would holler into his microphone, trying so hard to get it right he almost choked. I don't know whether the Muslims think it's funny, but if it had been a priest doing it Ashiq and I would have laughed just the same.

The call of the muezzin brought joy to our home, and when I thought about the events of the day before I was really very sad because we were happy in our little village, buried among the fields of wheat and sugar cane. Ittan Wali isn't very big. Farah used to say that, if you counted the houses dotted around outside it, there were about 300 families living there. The village looks like waste ground, all dirty and dusty, but it was home and I was happy there.

All the houses in Ittan Wali are the same. Their mud walls are crumbling and they don't have running water. But we were lucky enough to have electricity and to own our own place, which meant we didn't have to pay rent or worry about being evicted. Our house was pretty small, just one room really, with a small walled courtyard. That's where I used to like cooking in my big cast-iron pot. It was huge and always on the go, ready to boil water for tea or to cook rice. Ashiq, our four daughters, our grown-up son and I were happy to have this home that was all our own. I used to thank heaven every day for allowing us to live in peace, without the constant fear of being driven out or attacked.

It's not like that for everyone.

We often used to hear about Christians being massacred by Muslims. How could we forget what happened in Gojra, fifty kilometres from Ittan Wali? Everyone was talking about this appalling event; even villagers who weren't Christians were shocked by it.

Apparently, a crowd of angry Muslims went into the village of Korian and destroyed hundreds of houses belonging to Christian families, who were all living in the same neighbourhood. The furious Muslims said the Christians had profaned the holy Koran by tearing out pages and trampling on them as they left church after a wedding. Ashiq and I found this very hard to believe. It doesn't sound like the Christians here to provoke Islam, particularly after they'd just celebrated a wedding in the house of God. But the angry Muslims didn't stop there: the next day they were saying all over the district that Christians had insulted the Koran. So, to avenge themselves, hundreds and hundreds of furious Muslims – no one had ever seen rage like it, Farah said – attacked the big Christian colony in Gojra. They sowed terror everywhere, smashing everything in their path with iron bars, including Protestant churches. On the local news they said the police did nothing to stop the murderers, not even when they started setting fires. Everything that would burn went up in smoke, and not just houses either. Ten Christians were burned alive in the flames, in their own homes, including three women and three children. They died so horribly. When we heard the story of this murderous insanity, I shook all over and grabbed Ashiq's arm.

'Do you think that could happen to us?'

'No, don't worry. You know people round here wouldn't hurt us,' he had said confidently.

But I was a bit frightened all the same, and I felt sorrow and sympathy for all those Christians who'd suddenly found themselves in hell, just like that, for no reason.

Everybody knew this terrible story. The President of Pakistan himself said it was wrong to attack religious minorities like that. The Christian colony was just a heap of ashes and the Christians, who were poor enough already, were left with nothing at all.

Ashiq, the children and I were shocked and traumatised by this story. After that we tried even harder not to draw attention to ourselves. For example, when I was out in the village and I heard the muezzin, I would always rearrange my dupatta over my head so my hair was covered, to show that, even though I'm a Christian, I respect the religion of my Muslim neighbours. During Ramadan life used to change for us too. During the day we wouldn't eat or drink outside our own house. We used to stay out of sight so as not to irritate the Muslims, who are already bad-tempered enough throughout the whole period. Even Farah the shopkeeper, who was usually so friendly, used to lose her smile.

Ashiq and I understood the Muslims. It really is very difficult not to drink when the days are so very hot. For almost two months life runs in slow motion. The villagers are tired because they don't eat during the day, they feel crushed by the heat and they aren't allowed to have sexual relations. In the afternoon they often sleep instead of working. The village used to look as though it was all shut up; there was no one in the streets. The shops never raised their metal shutters till sunset. That's the time of the *iftar*, when the villagers get their smiles back. They prepare huge meals and invite each other over to break the fast. We were never invited, but that's only natural because we're Christians.

The period of Ramadan was harder for Ashiq than for me, because he liked to smoke cigarettes when he was at the brickworks. But he would stop, so as not to annoy his workmates, who weren't allowed to smoke during the day.

Sitting in my bed, I thought about the women who had

shouted at me for saying bad things about their religion. It was so unfair. I hadn't criticised their beliefs. But instead of bowing my head and saying nothing, the way Christians are supposed to do at all times, I had responded to their provocation by asking them why I should be the one to convert. For a Christian living here that's going too far.

When I was a little girl my mother told me that we were what they called 'untouchable', because we were descendants of low-caste Hindus who had converted to Christianity when Pakistan got its independence. I don't know how Christians in other places live, but in Pakistan, it's a bit like being an orphan in your own country. Even though the government has given us the same rights as everyone else, we aren't always accepted by society.

At home we didn't keep any crosses or icons of the Blessed Virgin, just a small bible hidden under the mattress. I can't read and neither can Ashiq, but that bible is our own little treasure, it is written on our hearts.

Dawn was breaking, the children were still asleep and Ashiq, still drowsy, was surprised to see me wide awake so early in the morning.

'What are you doing, Asia?'

'Nothing much. I was just thinking about what happened yesterday. I'm a bit worried; we've never had any trouble before. I'm afraid of what might happen.'

'There's nothing to worry about,' he replied, yawning. 'You're making too much of all this.'

After dropping the girls off at school, I decided to go and see my friend Josephine. Like all isolated Christians, we had very few friends. That's how it is in all the villages deep in the countryside of Punjab. The Muslim families didn't want to have much to do with us, except Farah the grocer, whom I saw every day and who treated everyone the same. The other villagers weren't hostile, but most of the time they ignored us. Luckily we weren't completely alone, because there was another Christian family living in the village. We used to share our joys and sorrows and we supported each other any way we could. I helped Josephine with the birth of her three children, and she came over to my house to do the same for me. There was a midwife two streets away, but she didn't want to help Christian babies into the world. I don't blame her. I know she was scared; she could have got herself into serious trouble. Josephine and I knew each other very well. For years we had shared celebrations of the big Christian festivals like Christmas and Easter.

Josephine lived just a few hundred metres from my home. I made my way down the potholed alley to her door, and luckily she was outside, hanging out the washing in her yard.

'Hello!' I said, trying to sound cheerful.

'Hello, Asia, how nice to see you! Come in and sit down. I'll make you some tea.'

Josephine was always in a good mood – unlike me, if you believe Ashiq. He sometimes used to complain that my mood would change just like that, for no reason. It was probably true, because my mother used to say that too. Josephine was taller and more solidly built than me. She had a pretty face and eyes full of generosity and mischief.

'So, Asia,' she said, holding two empty cups, 'how's things?'

'Not so good. I'm a bit worried. That's why I've come to see you. I want to know what you think.'

I told her what had happened at the falsa harvest: Musarat, the Muslim women, everything.

'Hmm,' said Josephine with a slightly worried air. 'It's never a good thing for us Christians to get into problems like that with Muslims. You know how they see us. You shouldn't have mentioned the Prophet. It's pretty much forbidden for us to speak his name.'

'I know!' I replied, horrified by Josephine's reaction. 'But they started it, with all that business about unclean water.'

'Calm down, Asia, nothing's going to happen to you. But in future be more careful and don't answer back, even if they have another go at you.'

'I promise I won't. Actually, there's another day's pick-

32

ing very soon. I can't afford not to go, seeing that I lost out on two hundred and fifty rupees yesterday. Will you come with me? I'm scared of going on my own and meeting those women again. They're bound to be there.'

Josephine thought for a while.

'Please, please say yes!'

'All right,' she said at last, 'I'll come with you.'

'Thank you so much!'

I was so grateful I clapped my hands and skipped around her little yard.

Five days later I was thrown into prison.

I found myself behind these bars, in this tomb, with no sun and no stars.

I realise I haven't seen the stars for two years. In the first few months I wasn't really aware of missing them. Then I realised that it isn't natural to be deprived of the moon and stars. I miss them almost as much as I miss seeing the daylight, the sun, trees and birds. In my cell it's like being in a well with no water. I'd like to be able to say hello to the moon and the sun, just once, to check they haven't hanged themselves. I'd like to look at the little beads scattered across the dark sky, the way I used to with my daughters on summer nights, lying on the *charpai* (that's what we call our woven mats) in our yard.

Since 19 June 2009, I've been cut off from the really

important things in life, the ones you never think about unless you're locked up alone in a dungeon for a very long time.

When I called at Josephine's to go fruit-picking with her, I was feeling fairly carefree. We each had a flask of water with us, so we wouldn't have any problems with the well. It was four days since my clash with the other women and, though I hadn't gone out of the house much, I hadn't noticed any difference in the way people in the village treated me.

As we got nearer to the field, I recognised the women who were already there working, and I panicked.

'Look, Josephine, there they are!'

'Don't worry, just act natural. Don't look at them and it will all be fine.'

I did as Josephine said. As we went into the field Musarat and the others looked up, but then they went back to work as if we weren't there.

'See,' whispered Josephine, 'you've got yourself into a state for nothing. Everything's fine.'

I've almost filled my bowl when I hear what sounds like a rioting crowd. I step back from my bush, wondering what's going on, and in the distance I see dozens of men and women striding along towards our field, waving their arms in the air. I shrug my shoulders at Josephine. She doesn't seem to know what it's all about either.

Then I catch the cruel eyes of Musarat. Her expression is self-righteous and full of scorn. I shiver as I suddenly realize that she hasn't let it go at all. I can tell she's out for revenge. The excited crowd are closer now; they are coming into the field and now they're standing in front of me, threatening and shouting.

'Filthy bitch! We're taking you back to the village! You insulted our Prophet! You'll pay for that with your life!'

They all start yelling:

'Death! Death to the Christian!'

I look round for Josephine, but the angry crowd is pressing closer and closer around me. I'm half lying on the ground when two men grab me by the arms to drag me away. I call out in a desperate, feeble voice:

'I haven't done anything! Let me go, please! I haven't done anything wrong!'

Just then someone hits me in the face. My nose really hurts and I'm bleeding. They drag me along, semi-conscious, like a stubborn donkey. I can only submit and pray that it will all stop soon. I look at the crowd, apparently jubilant that I've put up so little resistance. I stagger as the blows rain down on my legs, my back and the back of my head. I tell myself that when we get to the village perhaps my sufferings will be over. But when we arrive there it's worse: there are even more people and the crowd turn more and more aggressive, calling all the louder for my death.

A woman I can't see screams hysterically, 'She insulted our Prophet, she should have her eyes torn out!' while another yells: 'Put a rope round her neck and drag her through the village like an animal!'

More and more people join the crowd as they push me towards the home of the village headman. I recognize the house – it's the only one that has a garden with grass growing in it. They throw me to the ground. The village imam speaks to me:

'I've been told you've insulted our Prophet. You know what happens to anyone who attacks the holy Prophet Muhammad. You can redeem yourself only by conversion or death.'

'I haven't done anything! Please! I beg you! I've done nothing wrong!'

The *qari* with his long, well-combed beard turns to Musarat and the three women who were there on the day of the falsa harvest.

'Did she speak ill of Muslims and our holy Prophet Muhammad?'

'Yes, she insulted them,' replies Musarat, and the others join in:

'It's true, she insulted our religion.'

'If you don't want to die,' says the young mullah, 'you must convert to Islam. Are you willing to redeem yourself by becoming a good Muslim?'

Sobbing, I reply:

'No, I don't want to change my religion. But please believe me, I didn't do what these women say, I didn't insult your religion. Please have mercy on me.'

I put my hands together and plead with him. But he is unmoved.

'You're lying! Everyone says you committed this blasphemy and that's proof enough. Christians must comply with the law of Pakistan, which forbids any derogatory remarks about the holy Prophet. Since you won't convert and the Prophet cannot defend himself, we shall avenge him.'

He turns on his heel and the angry crowd falls on me. I'm beaten with sticks and spat at. I think I'm going to die. Then they ask me again:

'Will you convert to a religion worthy of the name?'

'No, please, I'm a Christian, but I beg you …'

And they go on beating me with the same fury as before.

I was barely conscious and could hardly feel the pain of my wounds by the time the police arrived. Two policemen threw me in their van, to cheers from the angry crowd, and a few minutes later I was in the police station in Nankana Sahib.

In the police chief's office they sat me down on a bench. I asked for water and compresses for the wounds on my legs, which were streaming with blood. A young policeman threw me an old dishcloth and spat out at me:

'Here, and don't get it everywhere.'

One of my arms really hurt and I thought it might be broken. Just then I saw the *qari* come in with Musarat and her gang. With me sitting there they told the police chief that I insulted the Prophet Muhammad. From outside the police station I could hear shouts:

'Death to the Christian!'

After writing up the report the policeman turned and called to me in a nasty voice:

'So what have you got to say for yourself?'

'I'm innocent! It's not true! I didn't insult the Prophet!'

Immediately after I'd protested my innocence I was manhandled into the police van and driven away. During the journey I passed out from pain and only came back to myself as we were arriving at Sheikhupura prison, where I was thrown into a cell.

Since that day I haven't left the prison.

I've been here two years.

★

The first time I saw Ashiq again I'd been behind bars for a month, with no visitors and no explanations. We were allowed to meet in the prison governor's office. We wept till we had no tears left to shed. I remember that, before asking how I was, he said in a low, serious voice:

'I heard you were raped by some of the village men. Is that true?'

'No,' I told him, 'it isn't. They beat me half to death and abused me, but I wasn't raped.'

Ashiq looked really relieved to hear this. Then he quickly told me that the children were well. It was my turn to feel very relieved.

'What about you, Ashiq?' I asked at last. 'How did you find out what had happened? What's been going on in the village since I've been locked up in here?'

The words came tumbling out. For a month these and many other questions had been going round and round in my head.

'When they attacked you at the village headman's house, Farah's son Zoeb came to the brickworks to tell me. He said you were in big trouble. I ran to the village as fast as I could and just as I got there I saw the police taking you away. I wasn't brave, and please forgive me for this, but when I saw that crowd full of hate I didn't dare go any closer.'

Ashiq hung his head. I put my hand on his to encourage him to go on.

'I was afraid,' he said, 'and I knew that if they saw me they'd beat me as well. So I ran away and waited by the river until nightfall. When it was dark I crept back to the house to see the children. Josephine was looking after them in the yard. When she saw me she burst into tears. "Ashiq, it's terrible, they've taken Asia away! They've accused her of blasphemy because of what happened at the falsa harvest." I realised it was a very serious accusation. I asked Josephine to take care of the children, because I had to go into hiding.'

My husband looked so tormented it broke my heart. Then he told me he'd left our house for good, taking the children with him, twenty days after my arrest.

They couldn't go on living in Ittan Wali. They'd had death threats too. Though they'd done even less than me, they too were seen as blasphemers.

Because we're a family, we're all condemned.

4

Death by Hanging

On 8 November 2010, after five minutes' deliberation, the verdict comes down like a thunderbolt.

'Asia Noreen Bibi, in accordance with article 295c of the Pakistani penal code, the court sentences you to death by hanging and a fine of three hundred thousand rupees.'

The judge raises his powerful hand and brings the hammer crashing down. It's still ringing round the courtroom when the crowd starts cheering at the verdict that will send me to my death. I burst into tears. I'm totally alone, flanked by two policemen who are clearly very pleased. I have no one to share my suffering – my lawyer isn't there and nor are my family – so I put my head in my hands and cry alone. I can't stand the sight of these hate-filled people, applauding the killing of a poor agricultural worker. I can no longer see the crowd, but I can still hear them cheering Judge Naveed Iqbal. 'Death! Death! *Allahu akbar.*'

I look up. Everything is a blur but I can still see the expressions on their faces, half hidden by thick beards, and the obvious joy of the three mullahs who have come specially to be present at my trial. When they stand up, the excited onlookers cheer them. I realise that all these people have got just the show they wanted. Then, a moment later, the door bursts open and the court is over-run by a huge crowd chanting euphorically, 'Avenge the holy Prophet! God is great!'

The policemen supposedly looking after me must think it's time to leave before things turn nasty. They bustle me out of the courthouse through a hidden door. Then they throw me into the van like an old sack of rubbish. It seems like the verdict has taken away all my humanity in their eyes. They even chain me to the seat, as though I've turned into a wild animal. They didn't do that on the way to the court.

As I can no longer move my hands or feet, I search with my eyes for a bit of window I can see out of. I know Ashiq is nearby, but however hard I look I can't see him.

★

When he came to visit me in prison a few days before the trial, Ashiq said to me:

'I might be lynched by the crowd if I come into the courtroom. But I won't be far away, I'll be outside to hear the verdict. Don't be angry with me, Asia; we'll see each other afterwards.'

'I know it's dangerous. Anyway, don't worry, I'm innocent so it will all be fine.'

Ashiq gave me a big smile.

'Yes, soon it will all be over, and about time too. You've been locked up here for over a year now. It's really good that the trial is happening at last. The children and I have already planned the party for when you come back to your parents' house. You know we can't really go back to Ittan Wali.'

I wept with joy at the idea of seeing my family again and leaving the hell of prison.

'It's a shame we won't be able to go back to live in our house and our village, but it's more sensible not to. I'd never feel really safe after the way people there have been so angry with me.'

For the first time Ashiq and I were happy as we parted. Without saying so, we both knew it was the last time we'd have to meet in this prison because, once my trial was over, I'd be free!

The hours that followed my death sentence were very cruel.

Securely locked once more in the miserable dungeon that I thought I'd never see again, I was devastated. Death by hanging – how horrible! And as if killing me wasn't enough, they'd also said I had to pay a fine of 300,000 rupees! I've never had that much money and never will. Why are they doing this to me? Am I supposed to pay to have myself killed?

Then I remembered something that might have been important. A minute before the judge sentenced me, I put my thumbprint to documents I couldn't read. I was naïve enough to think that, because I was innocent, I was going to be freed. I went over and over the whole story in my head, but I still couldn't believe it was all over. I am the victim of a dreadful mistake. If men are too blind to see it, my God and the Blessed Virgin know I've done nothing wrong, and that I don't deserve to suffer like this.

Holy Mary, mother of Jesus, I offer up my prayers and my suffering. Give me the strength to do your will. Guard and keep my children, my family. Keep us together under your protection. Help us in our misfortune. Bless us and keep us until we meet again at your side in heaven. Amen.

In my damp, icy cell I thought about all those people in the courtroom, Musarat's jubilant face when the sentence was passed. How can they rejoice at someone's death? Human beings need to get better, they need to progress!

Why am I so different? Why don't I feel pleasure at the sight of the sufferings of others? I'm not made the same way as them; that must be why they reject me, why they want to see me gone.

The law wants to kill me, but this death sentence simply turns the accused into a victim and the judge and his supporters into murderers. I haven't killed anyone and I haven't insulted the Prophet, so why have things gone so wrong for me? I don't know much about the world outside Pakistan, but one day at Mass I heard that a lot of countries have abolished the death penalty and that in those where it still exists they use it only for murder or for unspeakably terrible acts. But here, even when people are innocent, even when the accused aren't dangerous, it seems the only response is the death penalty. Capital punishment is the guardian angel of Pakistan, my own country, which not only doesn't want me on its land but also wants me to leave the Earth. I was so trusting; I was impatient for the verdict so I could leave this place that's killing me in its own slow way.

Two weeks before the trial I'd seen a prosecutor in the prison governor's office. He told me he was called Muhammad Amin Bokhari and he was there to help me. We talked for over an hour. He asked me to tell him the whole story of what happened on that accursed day of the falsa-picking. He told me I didn't need to be afraid, that it was a unique chance for me to have my side of the story heard and to proclaim my innocence if I wasn't guilty. He talked to me nicely; he seemed to be on my side. I trusted him and told him everything. I even told him that a few days before the falsa-picking I'd had some sharp words with the village headman, who is also the richest man in Ittan Wali.

That day I'd been looking after his water buffaloes. The job was paid 100 rupees and I used to do it for him and for other landowners. But that day, without warning, one of the buffaloes suddenly went crazy. No matter how hard I pulled on its rope, it refused to obey and go with the other five. It seemed to have lost its mind completely. I clung to the hemp rope with both hands but in the end the buffalo won. Despite all my efforts, I had to let go; my hands were full of tiny splinters. Then the mad beast started trashing its wooden manger. When the headman arrived he managed to calm it at once. The buffalo got straight back into line with the others, just like that, as though nothing had happened. The boss was not at all pleased. He told me I was useless. But it wasn't my fault his buffalo had gone completely mad and out of control.

'So what did you say to him?' asked the prosecutor, from behind the little glasses resting on the tip of his nose.

'Nothing. I just told him I hadn't done it deliberately and I apologised.'

He gave me my 100 rupees and told me to go, so I went. But the broken-manger business had upset me a bit.

'I don't know if there's any connection, sir, but after that, when the villagers beat me, it was in his garden.'

'That'll be all, Asia. Have you left anything out?'

'No, sir, I've told you everything. You can believe me, I didn't do what those women say. I've always respected the Muslims' religion, I've never insulted anyone, I've never had any trouble like this in my whole life, and I've lived through a lot.'

The prosecutor looked very serious. He wrote in a big book, in silence. I was physically exhausted by our conversation and shaken up by having to make the effort to remember all the details of that horrible story. If I could, I'd wipe the entire thing from my memory. Better still, I'd like to go back in time and never go fruit-picking at all.

As he got up the prosecutor said, 'It's good that you've told me the whole story. Now it's up to God to decide.'

Sitting on the rope bed that hurt my bottom, I wondered how God could have decided I was guilty of blasphemy. Which God were we talking about? Whether He's called God, Allah or something else, God is good and doesn't condemn innocent people to death. To think I'd been rotting in prison for a year, only to find myself waiting for them to put a rope around my neck. In my mind I could still hear the judge saying he had decided to condemn me to death after spending a year collecting all the necessary evidence. Evidence of what? That three women don't like me because I'm Christian? And then the judge dared to say, 'with no extenuating circumstances'. I may be uneducated but I'm not stupid. I know that means I have no excuse. But no excuse for what? Was I supposed to make excuses for existing, or for having a different religion? I really don't understand the justice system in my country.

Suddenly I heard a knock at the door of my cell and those of my neighbours, telling us it was exercise time. But I didn't want to go out. I wanted to be left alone in my black hole. I didn't have the strength to deal with more suspicious eyes and nasty comments. Horrible Khalil threw my cell door open with a bang.

'I heard the verdict – good thing too! You deserve to swing for the terrible things you've done! In the meantime, get up! It's exercise time.'

'I'd rather stay here,' I said very quietly.

Khalil's face went red with rage and he aimed a hefty kick at my bed, which overturned, tipping me on to the floor.

'You what?' he yelled. 'Who asked what you wanted? Move, you piece of filth!'

There were about twenty of us women out in the yard. The sky was grey – soon the winter would be coming down on us like an iron curtain. I was shivering. The other women were muttering to each other and giving me sideways looks. I realised everyone knew about my death sentence. They shrank away if I got too close, as though I might give them some nasty disease.

At one point, though, a woman I'd never seen before came up to me.

'Hello, my name is Bougina. I'm new here. What's your name?'

'Asia. But I wouldn't talk to me if I were you. You'll get everyone on your case.'

'Oh? Why's that?' she asked, with a confident expression full of goodness.

I hesitated, then I told her.

'I'm a Christian and this morning I was sentenced to death for blasphemy.'

'Did you blaspheme?' asked Bougina, who had clearly not expected a reply like that.

'That's the thing, I didn't! But I got tricked by some women who didn't want to drink out of the same cup as me; they thought it was unclean because I'm a Christian.'

'That's appalling! And they've condemned you to death for that?'

It did me good to meet someone in this world of death who reacted like a normal person.

The bell sounded.

'End of exercise!' shouted a warder.

Bougina smiled at me.

'Don't give up hope, Asia. As long as you're still alive anything is possible. Pray – don't stop praying.'

I gave her a little wave.

'See you soon.'

I was happy to have found a friend among the prisoners, but now I no longer knew how much time I had left to live. Bougina brought me some comfort by talking to me, being warm and taking my side. But, back in my miserable cell, I started thinking again about what was going to happen to me. I wished I could write! If I had learned, I'd be able to leave a letter to my husband and children.

I thought about them very hard and decided to write them a letter anyway, in my head. If I saw my lawyer the next day – though he hadn't been around much lately – I could ask him to write it and give it to my family. It would be my last request before my death.

My dear Ashiq, my dear children,

You are facing a terrible ordeal. This morning I was sentenced to death. I confess that I cried when I heard the verdict, but deep down I was not surprised. I did not expect either mercy or courage from the judges, who have been under pressure from the mullahs and religious fanatics.

Now that I am back in my cell and I know I am going

to die, all my thoughts go to you, my Ashiq, and you, my beloved children. I am angry with myself for leaving you caught up in all this alone. You, Imran, my grown-up son of eighteen, I hope you will find a good wife and that you will make her as happy as your father did me. You, Nasima, my grown-up daughter of twenty-two, you have already found a husband and welcoming in-laws. Give your father many grandchildren and raise them in Christian charity as we have raised you. You, my sweet Isha, you are fifteen now but you were born with a mind that is not quite all there. Your dad and I have always thought of you as a gift from God, you are so good and generous. You will not understand why your mum is no longer there with you, but you are here in my heart, in a special place just for you. Sidra, you are only thirteen and I know that since I have been in prison you have been running the house. It is you who takes care of your big sister Isha, who needs help all the time. I am cross with myself for having inflicted an adult life on you when you are so young and should still be playing with dolls. My little Isham, you are only nine and already you are going to lose your mum. Life is so unfair! But because you are going to keep going to school, later on you will have weapons to defend yourself against the injustice of human beings.

My children, do not lose your courage, nor your faith in Jesus Christ. There are better days waiting for you and when I am up there in the arms of the Saviour, I shall always watch over you. But please, I beg you, be careful, all five of you.

Please do not do anything that might offend the Muslims or the laws of our land. My daughters, I want you to have the good fortune to find a good husband like your father.

Ashiq, I have loved you since the first day, and the twenty-two years we have spent together are proof of that. I have never stopped thanking heaven that I met you, that I had the good fortune to marry for love and not to have an arranged marriage as is usual in our province. Our characters were well matched, but we cannot escape fate. Wicked people have blocked our path. You are now alone with the fruit of our love. Keep our family brave and proud.

My children, since I have been shut up in this prison I have heard stories from other women to whom life has also been cruel. I can tell you that you have been lucky to know your mother, to have grown up nurtured by our love and hard work. Your father and I have always wanted most of all to be happy and to make you happy, even if life isn't always easy. We are Christians and poor, but our family shines like the sun. I should so much have loved to see you grow up and get an education and to make decent people of you — but you will be decent without me!

You know why I am going to die and I hope that you will not be angry with me at leaving you so soon, because I am innocent and have done none of the things I am accused of. Ashiq, you know this, just as you know that I am incapable of violence and cruelty. But sometimes I can be stubborn.

As for my trial, it was quickly over. I was condemned to death in a matter of minutes. I do not yet know when they will hang me, but do not worry, my loves, I will go with my head held high, fearlessly, because I will be with Our Lord and the Blessed Virgin Mary, who will take me to be close to them. My good husband, carry on raising our children as I would have wanted us to do together.

Ashiq, my beloved children, I am going to leave you for ever, but I will love you for all eternity.

5

The Christian Minister

In my culture, wives can't read. The world exists only through husbands. But my husband doesn't know much more about the world than I do, because he never learned to read either.

We were both ignorant of things outside our village, but that didn't stop us being happy with our children and very busy with our work. In the evening, though, time would sometimes drag and, as we didn't have many friends apart from Josephine and her husband Samsoung, one day we took the crazy decision to buy a television in Fahad's shop. Fahad is young and resourceful. In his shop he sells old appliances from tips in the city of Lahore.

Fahad can repair anything, from ploughs to motorbikes, cars and radios.

We weren't rich. The money Ashiq and I brought in was just enough to make sure we didn't go hungry, to buy decent clothes for our five children and above all to send them to school. The state school in Ittan Wali isn't very expensive for landowners, but for us, 3,000 rupees a month was a lot of money. Ashiq and I always agreed we would do everything we could to give our children the best possible chances in life. We've always thought that if our son and four daughters were educated, when they were older they might get a good job in town – in an office maybe, who knows? When I was thirteen and doing domestic work in Lahore, Mr Akbar and Mrs Chazia used to have lots of guests coming to their big house. I would sometimes serve women who talked about their work. I didn't understand much of what they said, but it must have been important, because Mr Akbar seemed very interested in their experiences. I understood then that girls didn't have to be confined to domestic work, that they too could do things that were interesting to men in suits.

Ashiq and I want the best for our children and I think that's possible for my daughters, even if they are Christians. I want to go on believing that, anyway.

To escape our routine and buy the old television set in Fahad's bazaar, I took on more and more little jobs, like watching the water buffaloes and goats, to make the few extra rupees we needed.

I remember when the strange device that talked all by itself first came to our house. I still laugh when I think how long it took me to get used to it. For a long time it kept catching me out. I felt as though there were other people in the room apart from us. At nightfall we would happily turn on the television. We particularly liked the Indian programmes. It was amazing to look through this little window and see bare-shouldered girls dressed in sequined tunics, so pretty and beautifully made-up. I never got tired of watching them dance to the lively music. I could see that Ashiq was a bit embarrassed to watch these half-naked women. He would pretend to take no interest, but he never missed a moment of the show.

I also remember a film split into several parts. Every evening after the muezzin, Ashiq, the children and I loved to watch the adventures of Tara and her four friends. They had stormy relationships with their mothers-in-law, who tried to uphold the old traditions. We found it very entertaining and, as they spoke Hindi, we understood pretty much everything. (Urdu and Hindi are closely related languages.) The television also showed us what life could be like beyond Ittan Wali. It was like a new member of the family that knew lots of things. That little window lit up the outside world for us, even if I didn't much like it when Ashiq pressed the button and the Indian dancers vanished, to be replaced by the local news. The news was often sad and the images were very dull compared with my dancers.

Now I know that, if I'd watched the national news, I wouldn't have had to wait till Mass to find out that the government included a Christian minister responsible for protecting religious minorities.

That was in April 2009, my last Easter Mass, two months before the accursed day. Like every year, our family were all together in the church of St Teresa in Sheikhupura. I've always loved that majestic church. I remember one day I said to the parish priest that his church was very beautiful, and he told me that it had been built long before, in 1906, by Belgian Capuchin friars. I remember asking him:

'What's "Belgian"?'

He smiled and told me they were foreigners with white skins who had come from a country thousands of miles away to build this house of God.

The church was still decorated inside with Christmas garlands and the atmosphere was festive. There were about a hundred of us gathered there, singing our hearts out to celebrate the resurrection of Christ, who died on the cross to save us from our sins. I also remember the sermon by Father Samson Dilawar. He was particularly impassioned and asked us to pray for the minister Shahbaz Bhatti. That was the first time I'd heard that name.

The priest told us that this Catholic minister represented the six million Christians and three million Hindus who live in Pakistan. I remember thinking there weren't very many of us compared to the 170 million Muslims, but that our numbers mattered all the same. In his sermon the priest said that, as a minister in the federal government, Shahbaz Bhatti had kept up an admirable fight on our behalf. He told us the minister valued respect and dialogue between different religions, going in person to madrasahs known to be radical. We prayed and sang for a long time to help him in his struggles, particularly his fight to reform the law against blasphemy. According to Father Dilawar, this law was unjust to Christians, Hindus and Muslims alike, who were often wrongly convicted.

The priest's words reminded me of a story I'd heard the last time I visited my parents, in the village where I was born, a few miles from Ittan Wali. The people there told how an old Muslim man had been sentenced to fifteen years in jail for throwing away a copy of the Koran. But the man was blind. I thought it wasn't right, because he wouldn't have known it was the holy book. He hadn't done it on purpose. I didn't think that was blasphemy.

So we prayed for this Christian minister, a Catholic like me. At that time I could never have imagined that just a few weeks later I would fall victim to the blasphemy law, just like that old man, let alone that I would meet the minister for whom we had sung so much that Easter Sunday.

I shall never forget the day I met him. How could I forget it, coming as it did just after I was sentenced to death by the court in Nankeen Sahib?

I'd cried all night and by next morning all my tears were spent and my hope gone. It was all over for me. In the mid-afternoon I heard keys rattle in the huge iron lock and I thought my last moments had come and that they were about to carry out the terrible sentence passed the day before.

My cell door burst open and I saw Khalil's angry, menacing face.

'Let's go. Move!'

I walk down the corridor that usually takes me to the exercise yard. But this time it looks like the path to death – even darker and more crumbling than usual. I'm chained to the belt of the fat, disgusting Khalil. My legs are heavy, I'm feeling weak and, as I'm not walking in step with him, he drags me like a goat, obviously enjoying my final humiliation. Breathless, I watch him wiping the sweat from his brow and it seems to me that he's the animal, sweating like that. Then, as I walk to my death,

I forbid myself to waste my last thoughts on Khalil.

My children, in a few moments I shall stop living, but I shall be watching over you from above, when I am in the Lord's bosom. Dear God, take pity on me and grant me Your mercy.

The words echo in my head. With all my strength I concentrate on bringing my children and my dear husband before my eyes. I imagine them in our little yard, with our steaming pot ready to give them tea. Their faces are lit up; they are laughing with happiness. Isham, my youngest who's not yet ten, is humming a song she learned that morning in school. My other daughters and Ashiq listen to her in raptures. When she finishes everyone claps enthusiastically. Soothed by these tender scenes, I feel a smile spreading across my face when Khalil's harsh voice pulls me roughly back to reality.

'We're here!'

We were outside a door. Khalil knocked with a gentleness I'd never seen in him before and we stepped into an office. Two men in suits were sitting facing each other. I recognised the prison governor I'd seen the day I arrived, more than a year ago now. The other man I'd never seen before. He was dressed in a dark grey suit with a dark red tie, so he wasn't a lawyer. (Since I've been locked up here I've learned to recognise lawyers, who are always dressed the same, in a black suit with a black tie.) Who could this man be? Apart from my family and my lawyer no one had ever come to visit me in here. The stranger got up and came over to me (and Khalil, since we were still chained together).

'Hello, Asia. My name is Shahbaz Bhatti. I'm the Minister for Minorities and I would like to speak to you.'

The minister asked the warder to remove my chains, then invited me to sit down. The governor left the room and took Khalil with him. In my mind I heard the priest saying, 'Let us pray for this man, to give him the strength to conduct his just fight.' I couldn't believe I was now sitting in front of him. He looked like a good man who had a good life too, with round cheeks, a well-trimmed moustache and amazingly thick black hair, carefully combed and shining like silk. I'd never seen hair like it.

'How are you feeling?' asked the minister, sounding really kind and concerned.

'Not so good,' I stammered. 'You see, I'm innocent, and yesterday I was sentenced to be hanged.'

'Yes, I know, and that's why I'm here. I spoke to your lawyer just before coming here; he's going to appeal against the decision. That means you will be tried again, but this time by the High Court of Justice in Lahore. In that court the local people and the mullahs won't be able to apply any pressure. You can trust the justice system. I know you will be released.'

His words were comforting, but I couldn't help thinking of my family. I was so afraid something would happen to them. The minister must have noticed my distress because he gave a little nod to invite me to speak.

'I'm very frightened for my family. They're in danger too. They left our village a long time ago and my husband hasn't been able to work since I was arrested. They're hiding at the home of some cousins in Dingo, but my husband told me they'll have to leave soon because it's no longer safe for them in the village. They've received threats.'

The minister looked me straight in the eye and, waving away a fly, said:

'There's no need to worry. I've decided to take care of your family. They will come and stay with me for a while in Islamabad, until we can find trustworthy people in Lahore. That way they'll be able to visit you more easily.'

I was struck dumb by this minister who had come from the capital, Islamabad, just to see me, a farmer's daughter who'd never been to school.

'Is there anything in particular that you need?' asked the minister, getting up from his chair.

I didn't dare tell him I had nothing clean and dry to wear. That's not the kind of thing you tell a minister, even if you really need it. When it's raining outside it rains in my cell too. The floor turns to mud and my blanket and clothing get wet. I'm cold at night, but the guards won't repair the leaks. They seem to find it funny that it rains in my cell.

The governor and Khalil came back into the office. Shahbaz Bhatti gently put his hand on my head and told me to have faith and that soon he would ask the President of Pakistan to give me a presidential pardon so I could be released at once, without waiting for the judgement of the appeal court. I thanked him again and told him I would pray for him.

On the way back to my cell, when Khalil and I were chained together once more, he said nothing, seemingly annoyed that someone so important had come to see me, with the support of the prison governor.

In my cell my heart was light at last. I thanked God and the Blessed Virgin Mary for their goodness and generosity. I went over what the minister had said. It all happened so quickly! He had brought warmth back to my icy heart. Now I knew my family was in good hands. I felt so much better after our conversation, happy even, so that I danced around my cell with a big black fly that seemed to want to join the party.

I said the phrase 'presidential pardon' over and over, so I would never forget those words, which I'd heard that day for the first time. Two words that could save me and at last give me back my life. So my fate was to be in the hands of the President of Pakistan, Asif Ali Zardari. I knew his name because he was our president, but I didn't have any opinions about him. I'm not educated enough to understand politics. Everything I know has been picked up here and there, listening to my father and my uncle talking about him when we saw him on flyers and posters. Women of my position don't ask questions or join in discussions of that kind. It's only now that I realise what a shame it is that men think women don't need to know anything about things like that. After all, we are subject to the same laws.

So I didn't know much about this powerful man who had my life in his hands. I didn't know whether what my father said about him was true. But I preferred not to think about it and to hope that he would take pity on me and grant me a pardon.

That night I slept very soundly. The last two days had worn me out. My head was bursting.

Luckily that night it didn't rain. I was able to sleep the whole night through without being woken by the clatter of rain and leaking water that turns the floor of my pitiful cell to a muddy swamp. I woke up thinking of all the good news of the day before, the minister, his kindness, and the presidential pardon, a term I congratulated myself on remembering.

It was time for tea. I heard the trolley rattle down the corridor, the cell doors opening and closing over and over, since my cell was one of twenty or more. These sounds had become familiar to me: they'd been part of my environment for seventeen months, according to the minister, who had counted them. In a low voice I said the two words over and over: 'Presidential pardon.'

I wanted to believe in them. I did believe in them.

6

Happy Christmas

This morning I have a strange feeling, as though I have a boiling hot cup of tea in my hand and I want to sneeze. It's 24 December and I don't know whether to be happy or sad. In my language Christmas is *vada din*, which means 'great day'. But when I look around me and see my cell full of my excrement because Zenobia, the only female warder, hasn't been to clean it for ages, it's hard to think that today is a 'great day'. I see nothing but filth and I smell a revolting smell. I'm completely stuck, I can't go out, I want to break down the walls, destroy everything for a bit of open air. I'm going to have to spend Christmas completely alone.

Oh my Saviour, deliver me from slavery, give me the strength to bear this day that should be so beautiful, give me the courage to hold on far from my family and far from the house of God where I long to go with my friends and family to celebrate the birth of Your son Jesus. I beg You, Lord, have pity on me and give me the strength to bear the cruelty of my terrible situation.

I'd have liked to have a little cross or a rosary today, to celebrate the birth of Jesus. But I feel stripped naked.

Lord, I'm going to pray very hard all day, hoping Your ears will be open to me and that, even in my cell, You will hear that I would like to be like all the Christians of the world, free to celebrate the birth of Christ.

Lying on my *charpai* with my eyes wide open, I stare at the cracks in the ceiling. I put my hand on my chest, now flat as a plank of wood. My belly has hollowed out, my thighs have melted away, my arms are shrinking to nothing and from looking at my hands you'd think I was dead already. I'd like to cry, but today I have no tears left. I'd like to shout, but I can tell I've got no voice. My feeble breath is just enough to keep me in the world. I'd tear out my hair, but I like it too much to lose it. In this place I've learned how to die while I'm still alive.

The big black fly has just settled on my toes. It tickles. I smile and pull myself together. I refuse to die on the day of Christ's birth. I've lost everything, but I've still got my memories, so I'm going to celebrate Christmas myself, by thinking about the one we had the year before last. Back then I was so free and happy … Yes, that last Christmas of freedom is etched on my mind and no one can take it away from me.

For those of us who know Jesus, Christmas is the happiest day of the year, the blessed time for being grateful for the love borne us by the Father and His son Jesus Christ. There's no church in Ittan Wali or nearby, so with Josephine and her husband and children we all took the minibus to go to the Church of St Teresa in Sheikhupura. It takes two hours to get there. It was a special trip, because we rarely had either the chance or the money to leave our village. We were proud to be celebrating our faith in God's house, dressed in our finest clothes.

I wore the traditional Pakistani salwar kameez, a tunic with wide sleeves over wide trousers. That year I'd done as much fruit-picking and animal-guarding as possible so I could buy myself a new outfit specially for Christmas. There wasn't much choice in the one village shop, but I fell in love with that green and white outfit at once. As it happens, they're the colours of the Pakistani flag: green for Islam and white for the religious minorities, including us Christians. My knee-length tunic was a lovely emerald green, in thick, warm material. My white trousers were wide at the knees and came in at the ankles, just the way I like them, not too tight and not too loose. My long dupatta scarf was white too. There was no mirror in the shop, but I knew I looked good anyway. I was used to being in the fields all the time; I never got much chance to wear such fine clothes.

I'd sewn tunics in different colours for my four daughters: red and yellow for the young ones, blue and orange for the two oldest. When we left the house we had to weave our way between children playing cricket with a big stick and some old oranges, trying to make sure we didn't get hit.

One of the kids shouted, 'Look! They're like a rainbow!'

The girls and I all laughed. Ashiq and my big son of eighteen were dressed in beige salwar kameez that I'd washed and ironed the day before. They were also wrapped up in grey blankets and wore shoes. It's very cold at that time of year, not much above zero, but my daughters and I wanted to look nice, so we preferred to show off our colourful clothes. Anyway, we had the warmth in our hearts to keep us from the cold, though we were wearing socks inside our sandals. We had to be very careful not to get dirty, as the road to the bus was all dust and stones.

The bus terminal yard was bursting with vehicles and travellers. As usual for the trip to Sheikhupura, there was a minibus leaving within the hour. We paid for our tickets, thirty rupees each, then all took our seats at the back of the bus along with Josephine's family. I was crammed up against the window on the left, completely squashed by Ashiq, which made everyone laugh. It was 5 p.m., the temperature was around zero and the fog was so thick you could hardly see anything through the windows. As the bus rushed along the rough road we passed a few accidents involving trucks, cars, even buses like ours! I grabbed Ashiq's hand, but it didn't make me feel any safer. The driver kept his foot down despite the thick fog. Ashiq gave me a big smile and said:

'Thank the Lord for putting us at the back of the bus. If we hit something we'll be cushioned by everyone else.'

Halfway there the bus pulled up on the side of the road. Most of the passengers got off and went into a mosque you could just make out through the fog. It was even colder than before. While we waited for the Muslims to finish their prayers, we watched the car headlights filtering through the mist. We walked around to stretch our legs and the children entertained themselves by pretending they were stepping through cotton wool. Then the prayers came to an end and the little bus set off again. The fog was still thick.

The kilometres rushed by. I caught a glimpse of a tanker

lorry lying on its side and glanced at Ashiq, who didn't look the slightest bit worried.

With God's help we reached Sheikhupura.

The city was full of people – it was a big change from our quiet little village. The children were all excited, but they had to be patient because we found ourselves stuck in a huge traffic jam blocking all the roads around the marketplace. Nothing was moving at all: lorries, buses, cars, rickshaws, motorbikes, carts, bicycles, horses, donkeys and even pedestrians were all caught up in a mish-mash of tyres, wheels, sandals and hooves.

'What a place!' I said, turning to Josephine.

Eventually our bus was able to start moving again – and a good thing too, because Mass was just about to start.

As I got out I was approached by a man – or should I say a woman? It wasn't the first time I'd seen a *khusra*. There are lots of them in Lahore. She looked very beautiful, very nicely done. They aren't all like that – some men dressed as women still look just like men. I gave her a fifty-rupee note and the *khusra* gave me a blessing in a language I didn't understand.

Josephine turned to me and whispered, 'What was that about?'

I had a good laugh because, judging from the alarm on her face, Josephine had never seen a *khusra* before.

'They call them the third sex. They have their own

place in society – in fact they have more freedom than women. *Khusras* are invited to celebrations. When I was your daughter's age and working in Mr Akbar's home in Lahore, he often used to invite *khusras* round, that's why I know all about them. There'd be five or six of them at parties and the men could dance with them, because Islam doesn't allow men and women to mix. So this way everyone's happy. The men can dance with a man who looks like a woman: that's why they're accepted. But *khusras* are very poor and have to beg for a living. If you watch you'll see that everyone gives them something. It's a lucky thing to do, apparently.'

Josephine was amazed and I was very proud that for once I'd been able to tell her something I knew about. The children and our husbands were already at the church door and we ran to join them.

The Mass lasted at least three hours. We sang and prayed enthusiastically, full of inner joy. When we came out we could see coloured fairy lights decorating the roofs of the houses opposite the church. It was really beautiful and the children were filled with wonder. Christmas is the festival of lights, so little log fires are lit on the ground all around the square. Christian families gather round them to pray and sing about the birth of Jesus. While the children played and danced round the fires, we set out delicious things to eat on trestle tables. Most importantly, that's where we have our Christmas cake. Every family brings one that they've made at home the day before.

As usual, Josephine and I had made ours together. We'd started in the morning and, also as usual, we'd argued about the quantities, but in the end we always worked it out. By the end of the day we'd had a lot of fun and plenty of laughs. Our cake was huge, but that was only right to render homage to the newly born Christ.

Before sharing it out, I called to the children to come and light up the nativity scenes with little candles, and put gifts around baby Jesus in the manger. Traditionally we also leave money under baby Jesus, to help the parish priest, who lives entirely on what he is given by his flock. The children came rushing up, licking their lips at the thought of eating Christmas cake full of cream and sugar.

At that moment I'm torn away from my memories by my belly, which makes a very strange noise. Thinking about that Christmas cake makes me terribly sad. I know the prison isn't very far from the church of St Teresa; I could even walk there.

I hear the quiet click of a key in the lock. Perhaps it's Zenobia … Yes, it is!

'I didn't know you were coming in today. What a nice surprise!'

'I didn't want to leave you all alone. If there's one day to show charity it's Christmas Day, so I worked things out so I could come in to work.'

As I'm thanking Zenobia, she starts busily cleaning out my cell. When she's on duty she gives me plastic bags and a little trowel so I can get rid of this filth.

'What are you doing? That's not your job!'

'I can't leave you in all this filth today,' she says, collecting up my waste and putting it in a plastic bag. She's brought some scented disinfectant too. I'd forgotten the scent of roses even existed.

'You're so kind to do all this for me, it smells so lovely. Wait, let me help you.'

'No, no, you stay where you are. You're very weak, you need to save your strength. You rest.'

When Zenobia has finished tidying everything up she hands me a little packet wrapped in aluminium foil.

I open it like an eager child.

'It's a bit of Christmas cake,' says Zenobia. 'Happy Christmas, Asia!'

My eyes fill with tears.

'Thank you! Thank you so much. You can't imagine what this means to me.'

'Of course! Christmas isn't Christmas without Christmas cake and just because you're shut up here doesn't mean you shouldn't have a piece.'

I'm so touched by her thoughtfulness.

'You know today isn't a visiting day, but Ashiq called me last night and asked me to tell you that he and the children are thinking of you even more than usual and that, even though you can't spend Christmas together, he'll still be with you all the time and in your heart. Right, well, I'd better go. I've been here a while already and we mustn't get into trouble. Happy Christmas; I'll pray for you in church.'

Alone once more in my cell, now smelling of roses, I realise that Zenobia's visit has caused me as much pain as pleasure. A bit of joy in my underground life has reminded me of my sad fate. Until now it was almost unreal, but now there's no doubt, today really is Christmas Day. The piece of cake from Zenobia proves it.

Ashiq has left me a wonderful message. I miss him and the children so much!

The first time I met Ashiq I liked him at once. And he's told me he liked me too. He often used to come to my village, which was near Ittan Wali, because his uncle, aunt and cousins lived very close to my parents' house.

I remember our first meeting – I felt such a fool! I was in the toilet that my father had built in a narrow corner of our yard. A hole in the ground, some straw, an old black pashmina my mother had no more use for and, hey presto!, privacy assured – or nearly. Sometimes my brothers and other little boys would hang around outside like vultures. I'd hear their stupid giggling. To defend my private fortress I'd chuck stones over the top of the pashmina. That way I resisted their teasing and they often gave up before I'd even run out of ammunition. There was always a good pile of polished stones in our toilet. It was a bit rustic, but they were what we used to wipe ourselves. And they made good weapons when necessary – better than paper, anyway.

So there I was in the toilet when I thought I heard giggles. Without thinking I started to defend myself in the usual way, chucking stones over the curtain. But just then I heard a man's voice say:

'Ow! What was that?'

I came out of the toilet wondering who I'd hit and came face to face with Ashiq. I was so embarrassed!

'Oh, sorry. I thought it was kids; I'm really sorry if you got hit.'

'I've never been attacked like that before,' he replied with a wicked grin.

We both burst out laughing and the laughter stayed with us ever after. After twenty-two years of marriage we still have a lot of laughs.

In the weeks that followed we'd see each other here and there, but we never spoke. In my culture men and women never speak to each other unless they are married. If we happened to be in the same room we would look at each other long and hard, but only when the other one wasn't looking.

One day Ashiq came to my parents' house in military uniform. I was fascinated; I thought he looked very handsome. I listened very carefully as he told my father that he was in the air force.

Another day my family were invited to have tea with neighbours who lived by the river, but I'd decided not to go, so I was left alone in the house. Suddenly Ashiq appeared. He asked me if he could change his clothes before joining the others and I agreed, but in exchange I asked if I could try on his uniform. That surprised him – and made him smile. He agreed. It was the first time he'd ever seen a woman wearing military uniform and he thought it really suited me. He even took my photo. Where I come from, wearing someone's clothes means you love him: it's a way of telling him how you feel. Ashiq understood my message and he felt the same, I could tell. When I asked him to help me undo the buttons on the canvas jacket we were standing very close, closer than we'd ever been before. We didn't touch, of course, but I went very red and he seemed embarrassed too.

One day my father said, 'You're twenty now, Asia; you must get married.'

I panicked. Traditionally we don't choose our husbands, but I'd found my ideal man and his name was Ashiq.

My dad started talking again. My heart started thumping.

'You know Ashiq, the one in the air force?'

'Yes,' I said very quietly.

'He's the one you're going to marry. The wedding will be next month.'

It was very important that I didn't show my father how happy I was, or he might have changed his mind. I tried to look indifferent and just said:

'All right, Dad, if that's what you want.'

I didn't see Ashiq again until our wedding day, and I could see in his eyes that he was very happy to be marrying me too.

It was a lovely wedding. I wore a beautiful white dress and wonderful multi-coloured glass bracelets.

7

The Pope's Message

I'm woken by a terrible scream that paralyses me with fear.

Face tense, heart beating, I try to work out where the cry has come from, but it's the middle of the night and all I can see is the darkness inside my cell. I listen, but I can't hear anything, or at least nothing but the quiet sounds of the night. Then the animal scream comes again, followed by several long howls. My insides turn to ice as I realise that these endless howls are coming from the cell next door. It's Zarmina, my neighbour, who's screaming as though someone's trying to kill her. Her cries fill me with panic; they echo around the walls and seem to be pushing at the bars of her cell, but no one's doing anything. I seem to be the only one who can hear her ever more desperate screams echoing through the night. In turn I yell:

'What's happening, Zarmina?'

She answers with a yelp of pain. My voice isn't very strong, but I holler with all my might:

'Help! Help!'

I'm standing up, beating my fists against the thick wooden door of my cell, but all I can hear are Zarmina's desperate screams. I grab my iron bowl and bang it as loud as I can with a metal spoon. I feel like I'm making a hell of a racket, so loud it even blocks out some of Zarmina's screams, but nothing happens, there's no reaction. It's as if there's no one else in the whole world but me and Zarmina, stuck here alone in this prison. What are the other girls doing? Why haven't they woken up? What can I do? I look around me, but I'm totally powerless.

'Zarmina! Zarmina! Say something!'

But to my great sorrow Zarmina doesn't answer. She's not screaming any more.

I lie down again and, with some difficulty, go back to sleep. I don't know whether I can still hear Zarmina screaming or whether it's just her agony echoing in my head.

During exercise the next morning I find out that Zarmina has died during the night. No one seems surprised, as though it had all been planned. I decide to talk to the women in the neighbouring cells.

'Didn't you hear anything last night?'

'No,' says one and turns to one of the others. 'Did you hear anything last night?'

'Nothing at all,' replies the woman with a knowing look.

Then they start to chuckle. I seem to be the only one upset by Zarmina's death and, worryingly, the only one not to be in on the plot that was played out last night.

Zarmina was a Muslim, accused of blasphemy like me. Her story was totally absurd. She had just got married when she and her husband had a motorbike crash in Shergarh, several hours' drive from here. Luckily they weren't badly hurt, but when her husband lost control of the bike with Zarmina riding pillion behind him, it careered into a monument dedicated to the Prophet Muhammad. Zarmina and her husband were both accused of blasphemy and thrown into prison.

And now Zarmina is dead. She was nice; I will miss her. Why have we two been accused of blasphemy, my Muslim sister who died last night and me? I don't understand it. Have people gone mad?

Back in my cell, I'm still shaking all over at the thought of Zarmina's screams. I comfort myself by thinking about

Ashiq, who is coming to see me today. Then, like every day, I thank God for watching over me and my family, saying the prayer that my grandmother taught me when I was little:

Father, thank you for protecting us last night. Thank you for this new day and for the health You give us. Lord, be with us throughout the day, at work, rest and play. Fill us and all those around us with Your love. Amen.

My grandmother made me say that prayer over and over when I was a little girl, so I would learn it by heart. Today, in my wretched cell, I have nothing: no photos, no possessions, all I have are my precious memories. I've noticed that thinking about my childhood helps me to bear being locked up. To please my grandmother, whom I adored, I've never forgotten this prayer.

My grandmother was like a second mum to me – in fact I called her Ammi, just as I did my mother. I never knew my grandfather because he died in the war against India, but my grandmother often used to tell me about him. She said my grandfather had always been a good, kind man. My grandmother, my parents, my brothers and sisters and I all lived together in a little house in Kutupura, about ten kilometres from Ittan Wali. When I was five my grandmother started sending me to collect firewood for our cooking pot. Then, when I was six, my parents decided I should fetch water from the river. I knew the river very well. It took me just a few minutes to get there, but almost an hour to come back because the water jars were so heavy and difficult to carry. I used to go every day and I was happy to have that job. For me it was a chance to laugh and play with my cousins or the neighbours. We used to wander along by the river and splash each other – it was such fun. I really loved that river! I still love it today. I would really love to be able to go back there with Ashiq and my children.

We weren't rich. My father worked hard in the fields. He grew wheat, but he didn't own his own land. Every autumn he had to go and work for a rich landowner. He had the big responsibility of taking twenty sheep a very long way away, to Kabul in Afghanistan. It was an incredible journey that took several weeks along stony tracks. The going was hard and the horses had to tread carefully on the shifting ground, but the main danger was from the narrow mountain passes. On one side there were tall cliffs with jagged, razor-sharp rocks and on the other was a sheer drop. Dad's return was a huge relief to us all. And though my father was tired, he was glad to have earned enough money to see us comfortably through the winter.

Each time he came back he would take me on his knee and tell me tales of his adventures – Afghan villages with countless alleyways between mud-walled houses; wooden doors that opened timidly at the sight of a stranger; tanned, bearded faces topped by turbans; women in burqas who would suddenly appear only to disappear just as quickly. Though he was usually quiet and undemonstrative, my father liked to share his discoveries with us. No one from where we lived ever went to other places and, through him, the people who came to listen to his tales had the feeling that they too had travelled. When he talked about the distant capital of Kabul the women would gather round him like little girls, jiggling and wide-eyed with pleasure at the simple description of a new building with an electricity supply, a new road or brand-new neighbourhood that sprang up out of nowhere as he told his story.

Mum worked hard too, in the sugar-cane fields. I thought she was very beautiful. When she was within reach I liked to touch her, taking her face in my hands. She was full of energy, my mother: she never rested except at night, when we liked to lie close together. I didn't go to school and nor did my brothers and sisters. My father had said one day:

'You'll be farmers like us. You don't need an education for that.'

So it was my grandmother, with her wrinkled skin and aching back, who watched over us during the day. She was very old, but she didn't know how old – nor did Mum and Dad, though they did have a very vague idea. In isolated villages like ours age doesn't matter. Ageing is a part of life, like the passing of time and the changing weather.

We were happy together, and my two brothers, two sisters and I never wanted for anything. We always had enough to eat. There were chapatis and rice at every meal and we had chicken at least twice a week. We also kept two goats and a sheep. My grandmother was gentle and affectionate, while Mum and Dad were firmer with us. They told us off when we laughed too loud or when we played at throwing stones across the yard. Dad would go red in the face, grab whichever one of us was nearest and hit them on the legs with a stick. I still remember how it felt – it really hurt. We were very scared of Dad when he was holding his stick. Mum would always put the thick stick in its place by the bed and even when it was just lying there it really frightened me, so I would try not to look at it. My parents were strict, but they loved their children and were careful to ensure that we were always well dressed, so people wouldn't say we were poor. My grandmother never missed a chance to cuddle me. She would often take me on her knee and stroke my legs, humming a little children's song that I still sing in my head, to bring a little warmth into my horrible dungeon.

I remember very clearly the day I heard that Ammi was dead. It was during the monsoon, the day of a big harvest when my mother had spent a hard day in the fields. I was playing with some old rag dolls that my grandmother had made for me and my little sister Nadjima, when my mother said rather coldly:

'Asia, you're sixteen today and your grandmother is dead.' I was no longer a child, but I was as sad as if I'd been a little girl. It was my first big sorrow. Nothing anyone said could comfort me.

I think of my children, who must also be feeling desperate. I'm not dead yet, but it won't be long now. It's been ten days since the judge passed his sentence and I know I could find myself with a rope round my neck at any moment.

Nice Zenobia comes to fetch me.

'You've got visitors, Asia,' she says with a big smile.

I jump off my bed, over the moon at the idea of getting a bit of comfort from my husband. When I go into the room by the governor's office I can't believe my eyes. My two daughters Isham and Sidra are there too. Ashiq looks so pleased to have brought me this gift.

'My darlings! You're here! How is this possible? How did you get in? I'm so pleased to see you!'

Ashiq is triumphant:

'It wasn't easy, but Tahir [my lawyer] and I fought to get the girls in here to see you. And it worked!'

It occurs to me – though I don't say it so as not to spoil

the party – that this favour may be a sign that I don't have many days left.

'How are you, my loves?'

Isham, my little nine-year-old, says tearfully, 'We miss you, Mum, we want you to come back home. It's not the same without you.'

My throat tightens, but I refuse to cry.

'What about you, Sidra, my big girl? And how's Isha – not doing too many silly things?'

'I've had to stop going to school, Mum, so I can look after her. It's a bit hard because she asks for you all the time and I don't know what to say to her. She doesn't understand when I tell her you're in prison.'

'My darling, I know how hard it must be for you to take care of your big fifteen-year-old sister when she needs looking after like a little child, but you have to keep going and stay hopeful.'

I try to hold back the tears, but they flow down my cheeks anyway. Ashiq isn't crying, but I can see he's upset. My daughters and I all cry. To get us to think about something else, Ashiq claps his hands, stands up and says:

'Asia, I've got two pieces of news today, one good, one bad. I'll start with the bad news because you're still crying. You remember what the Minister for Minorities, Shahbaz Bhatti, told you about asking the President of Pakistan to release you?'

'Yes, it's called a "presidential pardon".'

'That's right. Unfortunately, there's nothing he can do. Tahir told me that the justice system doesn't allow him to make that kind of decision. So we have to wait for your new trial in Lahore, because the President has to wait for the decision of the Supreme Court before he can grant a pardon. Just think! Even the President of Pakistan can't decide to free you! It's unbelievable!'

I'm disappointed, but I don't want to dwell on this fading hope.

'Give me the good news then.'

'Are you sure you want to know?' asks Ashiq teasingly.

'Yes, please, tell me now!'

Ashiq takes a deep breath as my daughters look on, wide-eyed, then takes the plunge:

'Pope Benedict XVI has talked about you in St Peter's Square, in Rome, in Italy.'

I leap out of my chair and jump for joy, shouting, 'I don't believe it!'

At that point a warder gives me a sign that I should calm down. I sit down again quietly so the visit won't be cut short, and whisper to Ashiq:

'Tell me all about it. How could that be? I can't believe the Holy Father talked about me!'

'I don't know how it happened. Maybe Shahbaz Bhatti told him about you. Or perhaps it was because I've answered lots of questions from foreign journalists since the sentence was passed. Besides, you're the first and only woman to be condemned to death in Pakistan this century; that's why everyone's interested in you.'

'Do you know what he said exactly?'

'Yes.'

'So go on then, tell me!'

Ashiq and the children laugh at my impatience and I'm so happy to be with them that I'd like to stay there all day.

'He said, precisely, in front of thousands of people and on television: "I think of Asia Bibi and her family, and ask that she be restored to full freedom as soon as possible. And he added that he was praying for all Christians in Pakistan, who are often victims of violence and discrimination.'

'Goodness me!'

That was all I could say.

'You see, he mentioned us too, "her family". You're not the only star,' laughed Ashiq.

'It's so amazing. You see, children, all is not lost. We must keep faith. Our Lord is with us; He will get me out of here.'

Two warders come over to tell me it's the end of the visit. Before they chain me to their belts, I just have time to hug my daughters.

'I love you, my children. Don't worry, Mum will soon be home.'

Ashiq waves and gives me a mischievous smile.

Back in my cell, I still can't believe it. The Holy Father, the Pope himself, is thinking of me and praying for me. I wonder if I deserve so much honour and attention. Why me? I'm just a poor country woman and there must be other people in the world suffering just as much as me – or worse.

Thank you, thank you, God, for all the good You have done me today.

For the first time I go to sleep in my cell feeling happy.

8

They Kill the Governor

I'm woken by pain. My whole body hurts. My joints are aching, my hands and feet are swollen, my back is stiff. I feel like an old woman suffering from the cold and damp. Since my arrest I have slept on a single layer of woven rope, without sheets or pillow, wrapped in a worn-out old blanket. Winter in the Punjab only lasts about two months, but the January nights are the coldest. Since I was a child I've noticed that the temperature often drops below zero at this time of year. To increase my chances I've asked various warders if I can have another blanket. One of them said yes, with a smile, but the days have passed and I'm still waiting. I don't insist, so as not to annoy them, or to show them that it's important to me. They might take pity on me in the end, seeing me lying like a foetus with my knees up against my chin.

I spend most of my days like that, curled up on my *charpai*, trying to retain the little bit of heat given off by my gnarled, aching body.

Last night I was freezing cold again, but also frozen with fear. I had the terrifying feeling of being alone for ever. I could never have imagined that this feeling would take on new meaning a few hours later, when I would lose the little bit of hope that had kept me going until then.

That afternoon, 4 January, I noticed more movement than usual.

Noises in the corridor, rapid, impatient footsteps, each person passing knocking into a metal bucket that must have been left on the other side of the warders' room. Doors open and bang shut. These noises echo on and on, right along to my cell. I jump, to be answered by a metallic clang, then silence returns. These constant comings and going frighten me. With each footstep my heart beats faster. I don't feel the cold any more, but I'm overwhelmed by fear. I'm convinced all this bustling about is to do with me: they're going to come and take me away to hang me, as Judge Iqbal decided more than ten weeks ago. This fear that takes me over is so strong that I lose touch with reality. What seems to me like hours is almost certainly only a few minutes.

Then suddenly the noise outside stops and falls silent. I hear the silence of death, so thick you could cut it. I want to run away, to escape from this prison, but I'm turned to stone by this menacing silence. Kneeling by my crumbling cell wall, I pray I will stop hearing the sound that marks my end, this eloquent silence screaming at me that I'm about to die. The flesh on my arms is quivering, I can feel my face go pale, all my limbs start to tremble. I struggle to keep my hands together. I close my eyes.

Dear God, I haven't prepared myself, I'm not ready to die now. Grant me a little longer, let me see my children once more, hear my prayer. I am in despair.

A big black fly buzzing above my head brings me back to reality. I'm not dead yet, so I cling to this sound, which I'd usually find horrible, as if it were a life-raft. I tremble, and implore God to let me live.

Dear God, have pity on me. I accept death in submission to Your holy will. Father, forgive them, for they know not what they do. Dear God, into Your hands I commend my spirit.

Then, in the distance, I near a new sound. I listen. Thank God, I recognise the row made by the television. It's the theme music for *Geo News*. Joy pulls me out of my stupor. I'm reassured by the warders' habits. They always turn their television on every time there's an attack in our country. It's a sad ritual, but this time I think it has given me another stay of execution. The hours go by and the television blares on. It occurs to me that it must have been a serious attack this time. Night falls. Eventually I go to sleep.

Khalil makes me jump when he opens my cell door to give me my meal – my tin, that is. Khalil always gives me food as though I'm worse than a dog. Misty-eyed, I note he doesn't look the same as usual. He stares at me. He's about to say something, laughs and tells me:

'Your guardian angel has just been assassinated because of you. Your beloved Governor Salman Taseer, that Muslim traitor, is now bathing in his own blood. He was killed with twenty-five bullets in Islamabad for defending you. Good riddance! You'd better keep your head down!'

Then he bangs my cell door shut.

My heart trembles and contracts, my eyes fill with tears. I implore God: *Why?* Salman Taseer was a good man. He was governor of my province, the largest and richest in Pakistan. With its ninety million inhabitants, they call Punjab the 'land of the five rivers' and 'the land of the pure'; Salman Taseer was one of those. He wasn't a typical politician, he wasn't power-hungry and greedy like some, he was a humanist who was quick to oppose the Taliban and the Islamic extremists. When he heard about my death sentence, he defended me in public. He came to see me in prison and even organised a press conference in the prison grounds. That day I hadn't known that I would be talking to journalists and perhaps to the whole world.

The horrible Khalil had opened my cell door with a crash, wrapped up in a big blanket, thick and clean. I can still hear him saying coldly, 'You've got a visitor.'

I was surprised. It wasn't the right day for Ashiq's visit, and I'd seen my lawyer a few days before.

'Move!' yelled Khalil. 'I said you've got a visitor!'

His voice was harsh. I wasn't expecting it and jumped at his roar.

'Move! I've got other things to do.'

I jumped again, and couldn't help thinking that actually, no, he had nothing else to do. Jumping has been my main activity since I've been locked away behind these red-brick walls. I still jump at pretty much anything.

I quickly did as Khalil said, so I wouldn't have to hear more of his voice. With a brute like that things can get nasty. Before leaving my cell I gave a discreet glance around. My heart contracted. Whenever I left that putrid place, which I loathed, I'd catch myself wanting to get back to it. I'd come to feel at home in that tomb that was keeping me alive. Chained hand and foot to Khalil's belt, I immediately recognised the smell of the outside of the prison, a very particular, sickening mix of disinfectant and stale fat. As we walked down the long corridor, lined by around twenty cell doors on either side, my footsteps and Khalil's echoed on the frozen ground. I looked at the faded, yellowish paint flaking on the concrete. I'm not very tall, but I felt crushed by the vaulted ceiling – it reminded me of a crypt in a cemetery. A ghostly voice rose up from behind one of the heavy doors:

'You're done for, Asia, your time has come. You're for the rope!'

Someone cackled. Before more prisoners could join in, Khalil slammed their little windows shut, yelling, 'Shut up!' so loudly that it echoed round the prison.

As I walked into the unknown I realised that three months had passed since my death sentence. I remembered very clearly my visit from the Minister for Minorities, Shahbaz Bhatti, the day after that terrible event. He had made me feel so much better. In the days that followed I'd also had visits from a few local journalists. It was all a bit muddled up in my mind, but I remembered they all asked the same questions.

We came to a door I recognised. It was the prison governor's office. Khalil muttered something into his moustache, too quietly for me to hear. We went in. I was dazzled by a yellow light. There were a lot of people in there, making a lot of noise. A tall, heavily built man in glasses came towards me.

'Hello, Asia, I'm Salman Taseer, the Governor of Punjab. I've heard about what happened to you and I know that you've been victimised. I've organised a press conference, so you can tell the whole world that you are innocent.'

It was hard for me to understand that all those people were there because of me. I was frightened by all the lights, by all the journalists with their cameras, filming me as if I were some kind of fairground animal. I was wearing a brown salwar kameez that my husband had brought me the week before. At the suggestion of Ziba, a Christian Member of Parliament I'd met shortly after my imprisonment in June 2009, I was entirely covered, leaving only my eyes showing. Ziba is my ally. She'd quietly whispered in my ear that I absolutely had to hide my hair, so as not to provoke the extremists, who can't stand to see a woman reveal her face to a crowd of strangers.

I adjusted my veil and sat down next to the governor on a chair set slightly back. I was intimidated by all those people I didn't know. Me, a farmer's daughter, sitting next to a man like him … I could hardly believe what was happening to me.

The governor started talking at once. He told the journalists that I'd been unjustly accused, that the law against blasphemy was open to criminal misuse against the most vulnerable religious minorities, that not only was it against the principles of Islam but it did nothing to serve that religion. Then he stopped speaking. I understood that it was my turn.

I was terrified – I didn't think I could do it. Women of my kind aren't expected to speak at all, let alone in public, and certainly not in front of strangers. I didn't know what to say and started to stammer something inaudible. The governor quickly came to my aid. He interrupted me and, with a little nod of encouragement, asked me to tell the journalists what had happened in the village, with the Muslim women.

I didn't feel comfortable and I didn't speak quite loudly enough for the television cameras, but everyone listened carefully to what I had to say. Once I'd started I gradually got more confident. It was a unique chance for me to assert my innocence. I explained what had really happened with those women, who'd turned hysterical at the thought of drinking water served by a Christian; how, after the argument, I was chased by a mad crowd and beaten by several villagers who dragged me to the police station; how, once there, I was unjustly accused of having blasphemed and the police threw me into a cell, under pressure from the crowd and the village mullah. At that point in my story Salman Taseer thanked me warmly. I was relieved to have been able to tell the truth.

The last thing I could have imagined at the time was

that, three months later, that press conference would have cost the good Governor Taseer his life.

He even took the time to comfort me after the journalists had left. Before I was chained to Khalil once more, he told me to hold on, that he knew how hard things were in prison because he'd been locked up himself, in the 1980s. That was under the dictatorship of the much-feared General Muhammad Zia-ul-Haq. Even back then Salman Taseer had opposed the growing power of the fundamentalists in Pakistan. Later he'd become a businessman, then Industry Minister under President Musharraf, before being appointed Governor of Punjab province in 2008.

In my miserable cell, wrapped in my rough blanket, I watch the big fly settle on my tin of cold rice. I'm all tied up in knots. I can't eat a thing. If they managed to kill someone as important as him, what possible chance is there for me? How can I get out of here alive? I'm just a humble woman, a Christian, so easy to kill. I fall asleep, exhausted by sadness.

The day after the assassination of the governor, after a freezing, disturbed night, I hear from Khalil that he was killed by his own bodyguard. A few days later Ashiq confirms that the assassin shouted, '*Allahu akbar!*' before turning his sub-machine gun on poor Salman Taseer. The murderer had smiled into the cameras of Dunya TV.

The government has declared three days of national mourning, and that makes Khalil angry with me.

'It's all your fault! So you can go without your exercise today,' he rages. 'My shift was supposed to end at noon, but this official mourning period means we're under-staffed.'

I say nothing, so as not to make him even angrier. I daren't look him in the eye, but he goes on:

'Watch out! Just because you're locked up in here doesn't mean you're safe.'

Even as I'm staring at the floor I can feel him looking at me with smug, scornful eyes. Words rattle around my mouth, tumbling over each other like stones in a raging torrent.

I want to tell him it's not right, but still I say nothing. Since I've been locked up in here I've learned to make people forget about me: I do my best to fade into the dreary walls and dust of my cell.

When I'm alone again I try to think about all this, but it's hard to get my thoughts together. Everything is happening so quickly, it's all so complicated and hard to follow. I feel like I'm not the one living my life. I wonder sometimes if it's all really real. I want to keep hoping. God is with me, and the Christian minister Shahbaz Bhatti.

But now that Salman Taseer is dead, the Minister for Minorities knows he's at risk of being killed as well. I would understand if he didn't want to help me any more. Oh God, what is going to happen to me?

Five days after the governor's assassination, the warders Khalil and Iftikar come charging into my cell. I'm still asleep: it's very early in the morning. My body is aching, but modesty requires me to sit up. I sit on my rope bed.

'Get up! You're moving! The Christian has brought in new rules. You're to be held in a cell away from all the others. No more exercise out in the yard for you. From now on you're not going outside at all. They say it's for your own safety, but I'd be suspicious if I was you.'

I'm terrified. I manage to murmur weakly, 'Why? What's going to happen to me?'

'You don't understand anything, do you? No one here likes you. Everyone wants you dead. Salman Taseer was killed by his own bodyguard. The man who killed him is now a hero throughout Pakistan. And in here we're kind of your bodyguards, if you see what I mean. And listen to this: even the Interior Minister, Rheman Malik, said that if anyone committed blasphemy in front of him he'd kill them with his own bare hands. Your Christian doesn't carry much weight in comparison, so you'd better start saying your prayers. You can't sleep soundly just because the Minister for Minorities has got them to put you in solitary confinement.'

Dear Jesus, help me bear my pain, my loneliness and my suffering. You know I am innocent. Put an end to my ordeal, protect me and protect my children.

9

They Kill the Minister

Today isn't a day that Ashiq's due to visit, but this morning I'm feeling more lively than usual. On his final round last night Khalil shouted:

'You and Zenobia had better keep your heads down for the next three days. If you get up to anything I'll hear about it and when I get back you'll pay for it.'

Khalil never gives up. He's always got to be the hard man and try to frighten me any way he can. He's succeeded more than once, but over time I've got harder too. His bullying affects me far less than it used to. Sometimes it's even useful. I smile inwardly: Khalil would hate to think he was doing anything to help me, but thanks to him I now know today is Saturday, when the warders change over. Since I've been in prison I haven't had much peace and I very seldom have a chance to enjoy small pleasures. So I'm pleased to be rid of that thug Khalil for the next three days. Of the six warders I have, most are either indifferent or nice, like Zenobia. But Khalil does his best to make my life worse, as if it wasn't bad enough already.

So today Zenobia comes on duty. She will be watching me and running things over the weekend. Though my dungeon has no window and I haven't seen the sun for three months – after the governor was assassinated, I was moved to a different cell and I now live entirely in the left wing of the prison – luckily Zenobia is there to bring some comfort and a bit of light into my underground life.

Since I've been in isolation I never leave these four walls and no one is allowed to come in to clean. I have to do everything myself. But how? The prison doesn't provide anything to clean with. In this tiny cell, maybe three metres by two, there is just my bed and what Khalil laughingly calls my 'bathroom'. In fact it's a short water pipe attached to the wall, with a hole in the ground. But the hole isn't deep enough, it doesn't go anywhere and I have nothing I can use to remove my excrement. No human being can live like this, not even a farmer's daughter like me. The smell and sight of it are unbearable. Every day I have to dig deep inside myself to keep going. I fight to hold on to a bit of dignity, and that's where Zenobia really helps me, by letting me clear up.

We don't wear uniform in the women's prison. I have to get by as best I can with my own clothes, and that goes for washing them too. But in my tiny cell, without a window or a fan, it's very hard to dry them. The only place I can put them is on the bed, and the bed is also the only place I can sit if I don't want to get dirty from sitting in the dust on the floor. During the day, after wringing out my tunic, I spread it out on my rope bed, leaving a small space where I can sit. At night I sleep underneath it. There's nothing else I can do because I've got nothing to hang it on. But as it's always cold and damp in my cell, so most of the time I wear wet salwar kameez, which eventually dry while I'm wearing them. It's not very nice and last winter I was very cold the whole time. Now it's early March so it's a bit warmer.

I, Asia Bibi, have become a pariah and anyone who gives me any kind of help or support is considered to be a blasphemer too. That's what Khalil told me. I'm watched in my new cell night and day by a CCTV camera. Shahbaz Bhatti, the Minister for Minorities, insisted on it. I pray for that man every day. He had the courage and goodness to come and visit me a few months ago; he has kept his promise to look after my family; and he also ensures I'm safe, even in prison.

On 7 January, when I moved to this cell that's even smaller than the last one, I kept looking at the little box stuck in a corner on the ceiling, not knowing what it was for. I remember that, a few days later, I took advantage of Zenobia's being on duty to ask her.

'It's a surveillance camera,' she said in her quiet voice. 'It means you're safer in here.'

This answer didn't make a lot of sense to me.

'I don't understand. I often look at it, but it never moves. How can it protect me? It doesn't look like a weapon.'

'It's a camera that films you all the time,' Zenobia replied with a smile. 'There's a wire connected to a little TV in the warders' room, which shows everything that happens in your cell.'

'You mean I'm being watched all the time?'

'It does mean you don't have any privacy. But if someone tries to kill you they can't, because everyone would see and they'd know who it was.'

'I understand. I don't like the idea that I'm being watched, but if it means I can stay alive then it's all right.'

Later my lawyer told me that lots of prisoners accused of blasphemy never even get to court because they are killed in their cells before they can go for trial.

Now I'm used to it I never look at it any more. I just wonder now and then whether it's working and whether the warders really are watching me all the time.

Since I've been isolated here, I've really suffered from having no one else to talk to. If you believe Ashiq, I used to be a real chatterbox, but now it's a long time since I've communicated with anyone. In here I've learned that if you want to survive it's not enough to keep going physically. Talking and having some kind of human relationships, even with people who just happen to be there, almost certainly stops me from going mad.

I'd never thought about this kind of thing before, but I've noticed that the most ordinary things in a free life become really important in my boring existence here. I'd underestimated all the tiny things that gave shape to my days, like going to buy flour at the village shop to make lovely chapatis for the family. I miss my old life, and I'm so sad that I can't have it back.

I also notice that one of the hardest things to bear in my isolation is having nothing to do but walk up and down in my cell. Before I was put in isolation I used to go out for exercise every morning and afternoon. Now – and this is also for my safety – I never leave my cell. I don't see anyone else in the prison apart from the warders and

Khalil's bulging eyes. When I used to go out for exercise I didn't have any close contact with the other prisoners, but the simple fact of talking a little, seeing other faces and hearing their stories gave me something different to think about and allowed me to look at something apart from the filthy grey walls of my dungeon.

I often wonder how my neighbours from my old cell are doing. There are around a hundred of us women locked up here, mostly accused of adultery. But in reality many of them have been raped. Although these women are victims, they're regarded as guilty.

During exercise there were never more than twenty of us outside at once, no doubt because the prison yard isn't very big. I remember little Yasmin – she was only twenty-two. One day I saw her crying alone in a corner, so I went over to her.

'What's the matter? What happened to you?'

'I was raped, because my brother-in-law accused me of having a relationship with a man from another clan. When the news got out, my father refused to give me up and he helped me escape, but I was caught by the head of the clan. He kept me prisoner and raped me for a whole year. When he let me go, I gave birth to his baby, then I was thrown into prison.'

'What happened to the baby?'

'I don't know. It was taken from me as soon as it was born. I don't even know if it was a boy or a girl.'

An old woman sitting on a low wall had heard everything. She said to Yasmin:

'Your kid was almost certainly killed because it was a child of shame, without a legitimate father.'

'And I was sentenced to several years in prison,' added Yasmin, 'because the court said the baby was proof of *zina*, of adultery.'

I'd heard terrible stories of revenge and rape in my own village and I understood what little Yasmin was going through.

'Do you know if the man who raped you was punished too?'

The old lady with blue eyes and very wrinkled skin answered for her, sharply:

'Nothing happens to rapists in our country. They're protected by the law.'

This lady seemed to know a lot of things. I asked her to explain.

'It was in 1979. You're too young to remember the dictator Zia-ul-Haq. He was the general who brought in the Hudood Ordinance. It was a new law that made a criminal of any woman who had sexual relations outside marriage. At that time adultery was punishable by life imprisonment or death by stoning. Six years ago the law was relaxed slightly: girls are no longer stoned to death, but they're still thrown into prison for years, like you, Yasmin.'

A woman whose face was covered by a black burqa came over to us.

'I went to the police after I was viciously raped by two men who came into my bedroom while I was asleep. They used me to settle scores in a dispute between two landowners over a piece of land.'

'Yes,' said the knowledgeable blue-eyed lady, 'in our culture, and particularly here in Punjab, we women are often used to settle arguments between neighbours and tribal disputes. When it's not rape they burn us with acid.'

I noticed that the warders were listening to us. They didn't seem to like our discussion and were giving us nasty looks. The woman in the burqa had got into her stride and told us she'd been sentenced to five years in prison because she hadn't been able to provide four eye witnesses to her rape, as required by the current law.

'But that's impossible!' cried the blue-eyed old lady. 'If there are any witnesses at all they're threatened with death by the family, clan or tribe of the man involved.'

Nelofar, who's not yet twenty, has been rotting here for two years awaiting her trial because she became pregnant after she was raped by her uncle. She gave birth in the prison, but no one knows what happened to the baby. It was probably killed at birth.

Infanticide is very common. When I was twelve, my mother put her arm round me and explained that sometimes people killed baby girls because they don't bring in any money and are very expensive for families when the time comes for them to be married and a dowry has to be paid to the husband's family. I was horrified.

My mother went on, 'But Asia, we kept you.'

Listening to the stories of these women prisoners, I realised I wasn't the only one to suffer. From the beginning everyone here knew I was a Christian accused of blasphemy. Some Muslims used to give me funny looks, but they left me alone. They couldn't hurt me in the little exercise yard under the close surveillance of the warders. Usually I was happy just to listen to their conversations. I didn't join in much. My last experience with a group of Muslim women had brought me straight here, probably to stay here till I die, however that might happen. God knows what else I might have found myself accused of.

What should – or can – Christians say if a Muslim asks them if they believe in Allah and the Prophet Muhammad? I was brought up to believe in Christ, the Virgin Mary and the Holy Trinity. I respect Islam and the Muslim faith, but what can I say when they ask me? If I say I believe in God and Jesus Christ rather than Allah, I'm regarded as a blasphemer. If I say I believe in Allah, I'm a traitor, like St Peter when he denied Jesus three times. These are questions I never used to think about.

I haven't seen the girls from the exercise yard since January. I don't know whether little Nelofar went to trial, whether she's still here or whether she was released. I'm no longer on their corridor, we're no longer neighbours; I'm totally cut off, not just from the world, but also from the life of the prison. In my windowless dungeon I can't see or hear what's happening outside.

Ashiq doesn't tell me everything. He wants to protect me, to give me the courage to keep believing that I will get out of here one day. But Zenobia keeps me up to date with events linked to my case, which has turned into something of an affair of state since I was sentenced to death. For example, she was the one who told me about all the demonstrations that took place in Lahore, Karachi and Islamabad. It's terrifying to think of all those thousands of people going out into the streets to shout that I should die – me, a poor insignificant woman! Against my will I've become a symbol of the blasphemy law. So those demonstrations against me are about keeping this law, which it now seems no one can do anything to change since the governor was killed.

According to Zenobia the Jamaat-e-Islami is behind the demonstrations. The Jamaat-e-Islami is the oldest Islamist political party in Pakistan. It has existed since our country was created, with the Partition of 1947. I don't know much, but I know about this party because it was started in Punjab, where I live.

One day three young men from the Jamaat-e-Islami came to my village to find new members and expand their movement. Ashiq came across them at the brickworks. He was wary of them, listened to them quietly and made sure not to tell them he was a Christian. Luckily his Muslim workmates didn't let on. That night Ashiq came home late and told me the whole story. Their message was clear. They said that the Jamaat-e-Islami was campaigning to have the government apply Koranic Sharia law to the letter. The men from the Jamaat-e-Islami had said to the dozen or so men present that they were against the West, against societies motivated by money, that they wanted to restrict individual freedoms so that people would be better Muslims.

If Zenobia is right, there were 50,000 followers of these ideas in Karachi, and 40,000 in Lahore, waving photos of me with a rope around my neck and shouting at the tops of their voices in support of the law that says the punishment for insulting Islam is death.

Ashiq has never said anything to me about these many demonstrations, organised since I was sentenced to death last November. But Zenobia always tells me the truth, even if it's hard to hear and upsets me. I know Zenobia cares about me. She's on my side and she feels compassion for me.

The things that are happening outside are alarming, but instead of making me depressed, that gives me the strength to keep going. It stops me giving in to death.

It's still early and, though I haven't got much to go by, I know it's not yet 7 a.m. because that's when the warders bring me a jug of water so I can make tea. As well as doing my laundry, I do my own cooking, to make sure no one poisons me. The raw ingredients are brought in and I prepare them here, in my one tin.

I'm happy to think I'll be seeing Zenobia, impatient to look someone in the eye at last without it being interpreted as insolence or provocation. At last I'll be able to relax my face, let the tension out of my cheeks, try out my smile to see if it still works. It might sound silly to someone who doesn't know about my living conditions in this wretched prison, but that's all it takes to brighten up my day.

While I'm waiting for Zenobia, who will surely soon be here, I try to say a few words out loud, to see if my voice still works. Ashiq didn't come last Tuesday, so I haven't used it for more than ten days. I use it so little since I've been isolated in here that I wonder if my voice won't give out one day. I've also lost a lot of weight. My health isn't very good. My muscles don't work the way they used to, I feel less alert, and wonder how I can ever go back to the things I used to do – fruit-picking in particular is physically tiring and hurts your back. I feel like I'm 100 years old and, even if I'm one day released, I won't be able to go back to the same life. To warm up and see if my voice still works, I say my morning prayer out loud – the one I was taught by my beloved grandmother:

'Father, thank you for protecting me last night. Thank you for this new day and the health You give me. Lord, be with my family through the day, at work, rest and play. Fill us and all those around us with Your love. Amen.'

I'm glad to find that my voice hasn't changed and still works. Yes, I recognise it, it's all right, I'll be able to chat a bit with Zenobia.

And here she comes! I can hear her, I know her footsteps, the only lighter steps I ever hear.

She opens my cell door gently, as if she doesn't want to hurt my ears with the noise. In itself that's a kind action. She comes in and closes the door behind her. I get ready to give her my best smile, but forget it at once when I see her expressionless face which seems to be carrying the weight of the world. Something terrible must have happened. I don't know whether my heart is strong enough to cope with more bad news. Zenobia says nothing; she just puts the jug on the floor, still wet from rain that fell three days ago.

'What's the matter, Zenobia?'

She looks really unhappy. After a moment's hesitation, she says in a weak, barely audible voice:

'Shahbaz Bhatti is dead. He was killed three days ago.'

At that moment I feel as though someone has taken hold of my heart inside my body and twisted it. Fear freezes me, my legs won't hold me and I collapse on to my bed, gasping. I see the prison walls cracking and falling in on me.

'They killed him. A commando group of three or four men fired twenty-nine bullets at him. Our minister died in broad daylight, in his car, in Islamabad. The Taliban dropped tracts in the pool of his blood.'

I can't believe it's true. Khalil would have told me, he would never have missed such a good chance to hurt me. If it's true, why didn't he tell me?

'Tell me it's not true, Zenobia.'

She starts to cry.

Today Zenobia and I have wept together. She left just after this terrible announcement, fearing no doubt that someone would notice how unhappy we were.

So I'm once again alone in my horrible cage, torn and crushed by the unbelievable cruelty of human beings. My tears dried suddenly, but I still have a thumping pain in my head. I can't believe all this is really true. So many repercussions, so much suffering, so many deaths – it's too much for a farmer's daughter like me. Before this terrible story began my life was simple, calm and predictable.

To escape, if only with my eyes, from the hell of this new reality, I look at a little spider in one corner of my cell. It seems to want to set up home here, while I'm desperate to get out. I fix my attention on the spider, trying to create a moment of calm, get my breath back and forget, if only for a second, how dangerous people can be. I watch it busily weaving its web, delicately and with great attention to detail. The sight is soothing. Unlike me, this spider seems to know exactly what it has to do; it does its work without a moment's hesitation and seems so confident. This little spider doesn't seem to have any cracks in its world, while mine is falling to pieces.

I feel as though I've been in a waking nightmare for too long and the last glint of hope that still kept my heart beating has just gone out with the death of Shahbaz Bhatti. The minister knew he was under threat, the newspapers said he risked being killed, just like the governor. Ashiq did tell me that.

I've had no education, but I know all about the determination of religious fanatics. I know they always manage to kill people, yet, despite everything, I'm still surprised to hear of such fury and violence. I'm thunderstruck, shocked by the injustice of the minister's death. I think of my family. Who will take care of them now? Who will see that my young children are safe? I'm happy to die now, at once, if it means they can go on living.

As I watch the little spider going about its work, I feel anger and rebellion rising within me. For the first time since the start of this tragic story, I'm angry with God.

Lord, I have always been a good disciple, I've honoured You every day of my life. Why have You sent me so much suffering, so much humiliation and pain? Why did You take the life of that respectable man who still had so much to do to help human beings see the light? In taking his life, You have lit the furies of hell. Lord, I look for You, but I can no longer see You. I feel as though You have abandoned us. I ask for Your grace, I seek Your goodness and mercy, but all I can see are the flames of hell.

I look at the spider more closely, without going nearer so as not to scare it. It keeps weaving its web methodically and with particular care. It could go outside, but it has chosen to shut itself away in here. Sitting on my rough rope bed, I'm cross with myself for speaking so angrily to God. God is all love and can't be held responsible for human madness, for all the hatred in the world.

I ask the Lord to forgive me and to take care of Shahbaz Bhatti, to keep him by His side because he gave his life for a higher cause: he died a martyr's death. I remember a prayer my mother taught me when I was five. Our whole family used to say it every night before we went to bed. Today, for the first time, I feel I understand it.

Lord, come to the aid of Your Church and the baptised peoples. May they be faithful to the mission You have given them, to the word You have given them, to the commandments You have given them, so that, every day, they let themselves be led by Your grace.

I realise that the big black fly hasn't come today. It has been the witness to my little joys and great pains, but now, on the day when I've lost all hope, it has abandoned me. Maybe it's no accident. After all, if it had been here perhaps the little spider would have set up home somewhere else.

Zenobia told me the minister was murdered three days ago. I remember that day very well, it was Wednesday 2 March. It was no ordinary day: it rained continuously from morning till night, which is rare in Pakistan. Even in winter the rain doesn't usually go on for more than an hour, and it always ends with a beautiful rainbow before the sun takes over again. But that day the sky just kept on weeping, although we'd had nothing but sun and heat for weeks after a particularly harsh winter. That day it rained in my cell as well, as it does every time it rains, because of the leaks in the ceiling that still haven't been repaired.

Today I can still smell wet earth. I remember a drip that fell on my forehead and ran slowly down to my heart. Perhaps that was the exact moment that Shahbaz Bhatti was murdered. When I think about that day, I feel cross with myself for thinking it was less monotonous than usual. It didn't seem so long compared to the others, which all seem to go on for ever. But how could I have known?

The day before, I'd been visited by Ashiq. He'd been on good form. He'd told me they were going to spend a week with Minister Bhatti, to take part in press conferences with foreign journalists. According to Ashiq, the minister wanted to go on telling the whole world about my sad fate, so that Western countries would put pressure on Pakistan to release me. The minister also told Ashiq that he'd just come back from Canada and the United States, where he had talked about me. The minister had spent a long time talking to the Canadian Prime Minister, whose name Ashiq had forgotten, and in Washington he had even had a private conversation with Hillary Clinton.

'Who's Hillary Clinton?' I asked.

Ashiq looked like he didn't really know, but he said, 'She must be the American President, because Shahbaz Bhatti seemed very pleased with the meeting. He said it was very important to have told her about you, Asia.'

Tahir, my lawyer, laughed into his moustache:

'No, no! She's not the President. She's the Secretary of State. But that's very good too.'

I couldn't believe my ears. This very important woman had thought and spoken about me. She had expressed her support, and the Minister of Minorities had told Ashiq all about it, so he could tell me. Ashiq, Tahir and I were very happy about this good news. When we said goodbye I felt confident and energised, so much so that I thought I could hear music. I remember catching myself swaying to the rhythm of the raindrops, *plip, plop, plip-plop, ploop.*

I'm cross with myself for the good time I had the day the minister was killed, when I should have been crying along with the sky and praying for his salvation. I shall never forgive myself for dancing when the sky was so full of sorrow – tears of rain for a man who gave his life for justice and peace. A man who gave me his life.

I feel more alone and abandoned now than ever. I'm such bad news that even the big black fly has flown away. It must have realised it too might be killed through contact with me, like Salman Taseer and now Shahbaz Bhatti.

I'm tired. I feel weak. My eyes gently close. I'm just giving in to sleep when I hear the throbbing sound of my fly. But it has come too late. Now I want to sleep so I can forget, wipe away my torment, stop thinking about how I'm now at the mercy of the warders, who can kill me with impunity and maybe – who knows? – pocket the

500,000 rupees promised by the mullah. Before I lose con-sciousness completely one last thought goes through my head. It's the first time I think seriously about suicide. I want to leave this land of people who want me gone, to save my children. Too many people have died because of me. I can't bear it any more. I've decided.

Tomorrow I'm going to kill myself.

I wake up feeling terrible, as though I'd been beaten all night. My head really hurts. I vaguely remember having terrible dreams – giant, monstrous spiders taking over my little village of Ittan Wali, Khalil trying to open my skull with his keys. It's all a bit of a blur, but I don't want to make the effort to remember anyway. If I look around me, my miserable cell is already a nightmare in itself. There's no need to add to it.

I sit up on my bed with more difficulty than yesterday. My back is hurting more and more. My eyes are drawn to the teapot on the floor by the bed. On the lid I see the big black fly, standing there with a determined air, as if to say that, although it let me down yesterday by going off on its travels, from now on it will stay by my side. It's stupid, but it soothes my broken heart a little. I think of the little spider – a sweet little creature that took such care over setting up home in my dusty corner yesterday. It's nothing like the monsters of my imagination. I look for it, bending down to the ground as best I can, but it's not there any more and its web is torn. It must have gone. How lucky it is! I can't imagine how it can have got out. It certainly wasn't blown out by the wind, because there's no fan or draught in my cell. There is a ventilator above my bed, but it's very small, only just enough to renew the air in my dungeon so I don't die of suffocation. I wash every day with soap, but I can smell that the air is unbreathable in here, that it stinks to the point where I can smell my own putrid odours, wafts of decomposition, the scents of death. Perhaps I'm starting to rot like an old fruit, or fading like a flower that has no sun or water. At home I hung a little mirror by the door, but for almost two years now I haven't seen the reflection of my face. I feel as though I haven't seen myself for centuries. I do sometimes fill my tin with water and try to look at myself in that, but it's too dark to show me anything but the round shape of my head. So I haven't got the faintest idea what I look like now and, when I ask Ashiq how I look, he always says the same thing:

'You're as beautiful as the day I met you.'

Then I get annoyed with him because I know he's not telling the truth.

'I don't care about all that, Ashiq, don't talk rubbish! I didn't look like a twenty-year-old before I was sent to prison, so please tell me if I've changed since I've been locked up in here.'

But even though I raise my voice, my good Ashiq is always calm and gentle:

'You haven't changed, Asia, you really are very beautiful.'

But I know I have changed. I see nothing but grey hair falling over my shoulders, and when I feel my face with my hands, my fingertips touch hollow cheeks. My skin, once so firm and elastic, has become wrinkled and slack. My eyes must be red too, because they hurt all the time unless I close them. Yes, I think I must be terribly changed, and actually, even if I could look in a mirror, I don't know if I'd dare. I'm so afraid I wouldn't recognise myself. Basically I think I don't want to know; I prefer to think I'm pretty like Ashiq always says, as beautiful as the day I turned twenty.

I think about the idea I fell asleep with: suicide as deliverance, suicide to save my husband and children.

This morning I'm cross with myself for having such dark thoughts. I pray to God to forgive me and I know deep in my heart that He has. Our Father knows that a bleeding heart is never a pretty sight when it is sunk in a pit of confusion. With the death of Shahbaz Bhatti I feel the bars of my cell drawing even more tightly around me; I feel as though I'm suffocating inside these narrow walls that constantly spy on me.

I know I have no right to kill myself, because the minister gave his life for me. No, and I have no right to abandon my children, who are relying on me, and who think their mum will soon be home. And I have faith in my religion and I remember Father Dilawar at the church of St Teresa, who used to tell us that suicide was a terrible sin. Even though it's an act carried out mainly against yourself, our lives and our destinies don't belong to us. My life belongs to the Lord, I know, and if I'm still alive today, despite everything that has happened to me, it can't be an accident. It's because God has given me a mission. Perhaps, through my story, I, a poor uneducated farmer's daughter, can help others like me, and maybe save them from the death penalty. If I can stay alive, perhaps one day the blasphemy law will be changed. And even if I don't survive much longer, I have no right to kill myself.

So as long as I still have breath in my body I'm going to keep fighting to make sure Salman Taseer and Shahbaz Bhatti didn't die for nothing. I want the government to know that, even though they've shut me away in a tomb, I shall go on speaking out as long as my heart is still beating.

I keep thinking about Khalil. I'm amazed he didn't come by last night to tell me he was back and to taunt me in his usual nasty way. The minister's death gives him plenty of ammunition; he wouldn't have had to use his imagination. He knows the minister was my protector and that his death must have dealt me a terrible blow. But more importantly, today is the day of Ashiq's visit. We haven't seen each other for two weeks, not since the minister's death. He must be so worried about me. For my part, since I heard about the minister's death I've had a permanent knot in my stomach. I wonder where my family can be living now, since they were under his protection. I'm continually afraid, thinking what might happen to them.

It's early, because it's still cool in my cell. Ashiq won't come till around noon, and each minute is like an hour. I'm a prisoner of my routine so, to distract myself, I play a game: what time will Khalil appear? While I'm washing? When I'm boiling water for tea, or when I'm eating my rice to try to keep my strength up? He seems to be trying to make me feel uncomfortable, to keep up the humiliation.

This morning I'm really worried about seeing him. I've been very upset by the minister's death and I'm afraid I might burst into tears if he says something to me. I feel completely broken inside and, although the Lord has helped me build myself up a bit, I'm still very vulnerable.

Time passes and still no Khalil. I eat my rice, but suddenly I have a strange feeling, as though someone is watching me. Of course I haven't forgotten the video camera, but I sense a more intrusive, insistent stare. Sitting on my rope bed with my face buried in my tin to make sure the rice doesn't drop on the floor and attract every possible kind of insect, I notice a tiny window set into the door. I'm surprised that I never noticed it before. But I soon realise why not. The little window is open and, because it gives on to the corridor outside, it lets in a beam of light. I go up to look through it, but instantly step back, terrified by the sight of an eye on the other side, with a huge pupil. A bulging eye without a body. I recognise it as Khalil's and for a moment my heart stops beating, then the eye disappears. Now I can hear keys in the lock. Khalil comes in, looking very pleased with himself:

'Gave you a shock there, didn't I?'

I feel my heart thumping in my chest and I'm cross with myself for getting caught out again by his cruel tricks.

'So, your Christian minister's feeding the worms. Well, serve him right. And the same's going to happen to you. You're next on the list, you know that, don't you?'

I look at the floor and put my hands together to bring me closer to the Lord, so He will give me the strength to bear all these cruelties.

'Look at me when I'm talking to you, you piece of filth,' says Khalil, his eyes full of scorn. 'You'll have noticed I didn't tell you on Friday. I wanted the Christian woman to tell you, since it's Christian business. I don't want to dirty myself with your filthy affairs. Your husband is here with the lawyer. Get your nose out of your tin and let's go.'

So that's the end of that. I'm greatly comforted by the thought of seeing Ashiq. The door opens to the bars covered in wire mesh through which we talk. It's like being behind a mosquito net, except it's me that's the parasite. Every time I see Ashiq through this wire net I get the same feeling: it's like wearing a burqa, with a very limited field of vision. I've never worn a burqa, but I tried one on once. It belonged to my neighbour Fasareh and I put it on to see what it was like. We had a good laugh, because I realised that you couldn't see anything.

At last Ashiq and Tahir come in and sit down. Like always, Ashiq sits as close as he can to the wire mesh, but today more than ever I long to be able to hug him. It's been such a long time. We can only touch each other's fingertips. We aim for the same hole in the mesh but, as it's very fine, I can't feel the warmth of his skin. Behind the mesh Ashiq looks different from usual. It's dark, but he seems to have lost the little light he's always had in his eyes. He looks sad, and even Tahir looks crushed.

'How are the children, Ashiq? Where are you living now?'

'Since the minister's death we've been staying with Tahir, at his house in Lahore,' says Ashiq, turning to the lawyer.

Tahir is a Christian like us and, besides being my lawyer,

he's a childhood friend: we were born in the same village.

'Thank you, Tahir, thank you for looking after my family. I'm so afraid something will happen to them …'

'We were at the minister's house when we heard,' Ashiq tells me. 'I told you we were going to stay with him for a few days, remember?'

I was horrified by what Ashiq was saying.

'You mean you were in Islamabad that day and you could have been with him in his car when they shot him?'

'Yes. You see, heaven is giving us a sign.'

'Did you go to the funeral?'

'Tahir and I did, yes, but not the children,' Ashiq says quietly. 'Since we were still in Islamabad, we went to the official funeral at the Church of Our Lady of Fatima. The priest agreed to hide me among the singers in the choir.'

'You, Ashiq? In the choir? You can't sing a note!'

At last we can laugh. Laughter is so precious just now.

I would have loved to be there. I fire off questions: How was it? Were there lots of people there? What sort of people?

'The church was full,' says Ashiq. 'There were lots of people, his family, his brothers, his mother and nieces. They were all near the coffin, up at the front, by the altar. One half of the coffin was draped in the flag of Pakistan and the other in the flag of his organisation, the All Pakistan Minorities Alliance. When the coffin came into the church, carried by three of his brothers, there was a wave of desolation and despair. Hundreds of Islamabad Christians sobbed and wept; his mother was shaking from the depths of her soul; and some of the foreigners sitting in the front rows were crying too.'

'That's only to be expected,' I said. 'The foreigners are Christians like us.'

'The Mass was conducted by the Archbishop of Islamabad, Monsignor Anthony Rufin,' Tahir went on. 'We sang for a long time before the start of the ceremony. Later I realised we'd been waiting for the Prime Minister to arrive so it could begin. When [Prime Minister] Yousouf Raza Gilani came in through a side door of the church, there were a huge number of security personnel with him and, once he was in, the church was locked: even Minister Bhatti's sister wasn't allowed in. I heard about that when we were talking outside afterwards. The archbishop gave a very moving sermon; he said he'd thought of Shahbaz Bhatti as his son because he'd watched him grow up. Look, Asia, I took notes.'

Tahir unfolds a big piece of paper and starts to read very quietly:

'"He dedicated his life to Christ when he was still very young. He always saw his work in society and politics as both serving the common good and witnessing to his faith in Christ. In the work he did, Bhatti was doing God's will, he followed the life that the Lord had set out for him, with faith, obedience and hope. He always used to ask me to pray for him because he knew that, without help from above, work in the world is incomplete and cannot bear fruit. Without faith, political service remains arid and open to evil."

'This man gave his life for his faith. I'm sure that in the fullness of time the Church will proclaim him as a martyr.'

'At the end of Mass,' said Ashiq, 'Shahbaz Bhatti's body was taken by helicopter to Khushpur, the village where he was born, near Faisalabad. That evening, when we watched the local news, we saw that there were hundreds of Hindus, Sikhs and Muslims there alongside the Christians, honouring him with showers of petals.'

We fall silent for a few minutes. My mind fills with images of the ceremony as I imagine it must have been. Gradually I'm overcome by a great despair. I can't help murmuring:

'Now we're all alone.'

Tahir answers me firmly:

'No, Asia. We aren't alone. Shahbaz Bhatti has a brother called Paul. He has taken up the torch and he's going to fight on. I know he's seen Pope Benedict XVI.'

'The Pope?' My heart leaps inside me.

'Yes, and he didn't go alone. The Bishop of Faisalabad,

Monsignor Joseph Coutts, went with him, and the imam of the Badshahi mosque in Lahore, Syed Muhammad Abdul Khabir Azad.'

'The imam went too?' It's one surprise after another.

Ashiq says nothing, but a timid smile appears on his lips.

'Yes, the imam went too. He's a brave man. That's why we mustn't give up hope. You must stay strong, Asia. You are not alone.'

Afterword

I'm scared. Since the murder of the minister I've been racked by a terrible fear. I'm waiting for the time that God will take me to Him, the way you wait for an oasis in the desert. I'm exhausted. I need to rest. But I don't think people can set themselves in God's place and decide when another human being will die. When my time comes, I will accept it.

The one thing that keeps me going, despite all the deprivation, anger and this terrible fear that never leaves me, is the certainty that I am innocent. The certainty that I am being treated unjustly. And the desire to bear witness, to do what I can so that my fight will help other people. I've got no education, I've always lived very simply, but today I think perhaps my life will have an impact on the life of my country.

★

Every day since the death of Shahbaz Bhatti, I've been afraid that the man who is going to put me to death will step into my cell. I'm no longer protected by the minister's benevolence. But I know that others have taken up the baton. Foreigners who have been moved by my fate, and people in my own country too.

I tell myself these things to give me courage. And I think about my family. My husband standing firm beside me, my children … My darlings, whom I haven't seen for so long. My heart is warmed by the thought that they are all still alive, despite the threats hanging over them. I would give my life ten times over if I could be certain it would save them. I want them to be happy, to find the peace they have not felt since I've been in prison. Whatever happens, I want them to be able to build lives for themselves and to pass on all the love I feel for them. They are like seeds of hope and love, and I hope they will grow and flourish.

So now you know a bit more about me, it's you I want to speak to. You've read my story and you've learned about my country, our life that's happy in spite of everything – or could be. I'm just one woman among all the very many women of this world, but I humbly believe that my suffering is like that of others. I long for my persecutors' eyes to be opened, for the situation in my country to change.

Now that you know my story, tell other people you

know about what has happened to me. Spread the word. I believe this is the only chance I have of not dying in this dungeon.

I need you. Help me.

Sheikhupura prison
April 2011